CLOUDLAND REVISITED

S. J. Perelman

CLOUDLAND REVISITED

A Misspent Youth in Books and Film

With an Introduction by Adam Gopnik

LIBRARY OF AMERICA

Distributed to the trade in the United States by Penguin Random House Inc.
and in Canada by Penguin Random House Canada Ltd.

Library of Congress Control Number: 2023939522
ISBN 978–1–59853–780–2

1 3 5 7 9 10 8 6 4 2

Printed in the United States of America

Contents

Introduction

BY ADAM GOPNIK

BIG BOOKS get made when fault lines break and crevasses in consciousness spring open, through wars and plagues and occupations. A *War and Peace* takes war, and peace. Great comic literature sits on historical fault lines too, but usually at moments when we can just begin to feel the earth move and hear, as a very distant rumble, the trembling of the plates. Molière's comedies, for instance, are set within a confident aristocratic society and an absolutist court with strict rules and manners about fidelity, loyalty, and courtesy—but at a time when that arrangement was just beginning to be shaken by, and slip away from, a middle-class society with its own cult of candor and sincerity. Mark Twain made the greatest American comic novel by writing backwards, so to speak, to a moment when the great earthquake of *his* time, the Civil War, had not yet taken place, but was already in motion. In our own era, Steve Martin drew his juice and energy from the way that all the rituals of traditional show business as they had stood since vaudeville, were disassembling and suddenly could only be imagined ironically, so that being "entertaining" was in itself a form of being ridiculous.

S. J. Perelman's "Cloudland Revisited" series, written in the 1940s and '50s as a suite of pieces for *The New Yorker*, and in this volume reprinted in full for the first time, though irresistible as a tour de force of American language—filled with those astonishing Perelman sentences where nineteenth century circumlocution crashes head-on into twentieth-century demotic while a crowd of rubbernecking publicity agents and advertising writers look on—sits on another fault line between shifting attitudes to pop entertainment in America. Undertaken in a purely mocking vein as a study of the pulp fiction and silent movies that had held him in thrall as an adolescent, it devolves into a fascinated and affectionate one—and ends, for readers now, as a kind of working catalogue, sparkling rather than academic, of how American consciousness gets made from the birdcage lining of pop culture in our heads. Before any post-modern critic, Perelman gave us a green baize bag with among its contents, "a copy of Caesar's Gallic commentaries, a half-eaten jelly sandwich, and a newspaper advertisement announcing the première that afternoon at the Victory of Cecil B. DeMille's newest epic, *Male and Female*." He understood how Latin diction ran into silent movie absurdities through, so to speak, the intermediary of a jelly sandwich. As much as Scott Fitzgerald's *The Crack-Up*—which also began life as a suite of "casual" magazine pieces—set the pattern for the American confessional, Perelman's "Cloudland" series set the pattern for the American pop-art memoir, of the kind where a literary life is revealed through its engagement not with the high culture of its time but in a kind of meta-tussle with its mass-market overcharge, in a tone by turns affectionate, exasperated, nostalgic, and ironic.

Perelman began the "Cloudland" series in the late '40s, as he approached the height of his own powers and reputation and kept at it into the mid-'50s—among his most productive and, from a sentence-by-sentence vantage point, certainly his most radiant decade. It was the moment when he distanced himself from the pack of *New Yorker* "casual" writers to become celebrated as the best of the bunch, surpassing the increasingly long-winded Thurber, with Dorothy Parker announcing, in 1957, and in *The New York Times*, that he stood alone among American humorists; he would even win, in those years, what he would have called, in hard-breathing and jeering italics, the ultimate accolade, an Oscar for Best Adapted Screenplay in that same year, 1957, for what now seems the stiffly written or, at least, stiffly played, Mike Todd spectacle *Around the World in 80 Days*.

Series of this kind were a feature of *New Yorker* comedy-writing then, as they are no more—Frank Sullivan's "Cliché Expert," who "testified" regularly on the bromides of countless issues is a prime instance. Ideas are the most valued currency of a humorist's life and Perelman, looking for his own self-renewing subject, saw the potential of the cheap fiction that had engaged him as a boy and enraged him now.

The style of the pieces is set early: Sid recalls in lovingly detailed self-mockery the condition he had been in as a boy in Providence Rhode Island when he first encountered the book or film and the effect it had on him—from barricading his bedroom against the entry of the evil Dr. Fu Manchu to imitating the sneer of Eric Von Stroheim—and then revisits it in a note of self-mocking wonder that even a bright adolescent could have been so stirred by the thing, with the parallel understanding that in some odd way or another it is still stirring his older self now.

By "Cloudland" he meant the condition of semi-innocence— "semi" since it was illuminated throughout by adolescent lust—in which he first encountered the books, and then the movies, he would write about. Simply describing their plots and performances would both recapture the rococo absurdities of American pop culture in the teens and twenties, already distant and "vintage" by the late 1940s—cf. *Sunset Boulevard*, where a woman in her fifties, a star a mere twenty-five years before, is a long-forgotten grotesque—and serve as a kind of memoir of sensibility, then and now. The counterpoint between the hard-boiled Big Sid who's seen it all, and the younger Little Sid, who's seen nothing but the movies, would make the comedy.

*

Sid's silent movie stuff is so memorable—having read it first around the age of thirteen, I find descriptive sentences and paragraphs still lingering firmly in mind—that it is a little startling to be reminded that the series began as one strictly devoted to the dime novels that the young Sid had read in between trips to the theater. Sax Rohmer's *The Mystery of Dr. Fu-Manchu* and Elinor Glyn's *Three Weeks*; the original Edgar Rice Burroughs *Tarzan of the Apes* and some still more forgotten semi-lewd classics of the period, including *Leonie of the Jungle* by Joan Conquest and Cyril Hume's *Wife of the Centaur*. (It's hard to believe that both "Cyril Hume" and *Wife of the Centaur* are not names dreamt up by Perelman, but they're not.)

The contemporary reader delights in the narrow-eyed scrutiny Perelman gives to the literary conventions thereby entombed, as when he writes, of one of the heroes of the Fu Manchu cycle that "The alacrity with which doctors of that epoch deserted their practice has never ceased to impress me. Holmes had only to crook his finger and Watson went bowling away in a four-wheeler, leaving his patients to fend for themselves. If the foregoing is at all indicative, the mortality rate of London in the 1900s must have been appalling; the average physician seems to have spent much less time in diagnosis than in tiptoeing around Wapping Old Stairs with a dark lantern."

The perfection of Perelman's memory for a specific vocabulary— "Wapping Old Stairs and with a dark lantern"—is matched only by his ability to load a long sentence with varied verbal shot and still make it go off with a single neat "Bang!": "With puff adders, tarantulas, and highbinders blooming in every hedgerow, the hole-and-corner pursuit of Fu-Manchu drums along through the next hundred pages at about the same tempo, resolutely shying away from climaxes like Hindus from meat."

The series is specifically keyed to that decade when Perelman was eleven to twenty-one, by far the most impressionable and important in any writer's life, the decade that marks passage from boyhood or girlhood to some kind of precarious adulthood, with the long way lit by passion. Indeed, the erotic education of an American youngster, as it has taken place ever since—through the sublimation and titillation of sex into mass entertainment, with just enough to excite a kid and not too much to offend the censor overseeing the kid's entertainments—turns out to be the key motif of the series. His exquisite evocation of the whole negligee and neck-kissing world of the silent film is one of the most consistently funny things he satirizes. In one of his pieces, Perelman recalls the mood that gripped him for a full month after seeing his first Theda Bara movie (Theda Bara, born in Cincinnati but presented to the Perelman generation as an Egyptian "vamp," the first of the long line of American sex symbols with screen lives briefer than ghost moths): "I gave myself up to fantasies in which I lay with my head pillowed in the seductress's lap, intoxicated by coal-black eyes smoldering with belladonna. At her bidding, I eschewed family, social position, my brilliant career—a rather hazy combination of African explorer and private sleuth—to follow her to the ends of the earth. I saw myself, oblivious of everything but the nectar of her lips, being cashiered for cheating at cards (I was also a major in the Horse Dragoons), descending to drugs, and ultimately winding up as a beachcomber in the South Seas, with a saintly, ascetic face like H. B. Warner's." (Once one begins quoting Perelman, the problem is where to stop!)

Yet note, at least in passing, as well two more essential Perelman truths in the passage above: first the credibility of the adolescent fantasy—and then the Anglophilia that illuminates it all. Perelman knew early on what the horse dragoons might be, and that they might be more susceptible to cheating scandals than another regiment, while his scenario of pained beachcomber resignation comes right out of Somerset Maugham, a key negative influence on him, i.e., someone whose affectations he respected and mocked in equal parts. Toward the end of his life he made a failed attempt at being an English gentleman in London. "I expected kindness and gentility and I found it, but there is such a thing as too much couth," he announced memorably afterward, but the fantasy was deeply rooted in his providential past.

*

Delightful, and lovingly absurd, as the passages on pulp fiction are it is in the sessions devoted to silent movies that Perelman shines brightest. The reasons for this, sheer practice and increasing confidence aside, are manifold. First, it involved some unusually disciplined reporting, for a humorist; the silent-film division of the "Cloudland" project demanded a new kind of purpose. He wrote to his confidante Lela Hadley that "I've spent almost all the past two weeks at the Museum of Modern Art projecting ten films I plan to write about in the Cloudland Revisited series in *The New Yorker*, things I saw between 1915 and 1925—*Foolish Wives* (von Stroheim), *20,000 Leagues under the Sea, Way Down East, Male and Female, Excuse My Dust, Stella Dallas*, etc. The museum's film division was extremely co-operative; I'd been trying to set up this scheme for about two years and had been at some pains to figure out where I could uncover the particular films I wanted, as they've large disappeared. . . . I worked with a tape recorder while the films were being shown, talking into it and describing the contents of each scene and the subtitles. I now have the secretary in the adjoining office transcribing the tape." (Though one would give a lot to have the tapes of that mumbled Perelman narration, in truth little of an oral "sound" penetrates his sentences. Sid wrote like Sid, whatever the source of the writing.)

A still deeper reason for the superiority of the movie stuff to the wonderful book stuff is simply that the movies occupied then, as they do now, a more central and fraught place in American life than does old boudoir and adventure fiction. The Museum of Modern Art, as that letter reveals, had already begun collecting old movies, and so Perelman's project—mocking the defunct absurdities of the movies he recalled—depended ironically on the scholarly enterprise in preserving them. Although film had been part of the MoMA collection from early on, it would have been far from self-evident to anyone in the 1930s, as the museum came together under its first director, Alfred H. Barr Jr., that commercial, Hollywood movies, would come to have such a significant place there as they already had by the '50s. Though the collection had a comprehensive bent from early on, it seems to have only latterly, if presciently, recognized that Hollywood movies, of the kind usually dismissed as "kitsch" by the same people who came to see abstract painting, were a necessity.

And then the period under scrutiny was tightly sealed, by chance, by the fact that, where popular and pulp fiction had remained more or less fixed in its course from the '20s on, with "hard boiled" private eyes taking over from the leaping libidinal centaurs, over the period of Perelman's adolescence silent films had first fully blossomed and then entirely died—giving his recollection of them an absolute, sealed-off King Tut's tomb quality. They were past in ways the books were not. (Literally so—almost none of Theda Bara's movies survive at all, after nitrate fires.)

A few interlinked notes of social history inflect—perhaps unconsciously, certainly richly—Perelman's project. First, thirty to forty years past is always the prime site of American nostalgia, and Perelman in the '40s and '50s was participating in a general "revival" of the popular art of the teens and '20s. Just as the aughts in the current century saw a fascination with the style of the 1960s, as in *Madmen,* and the '70s was obsessed with thirties movies and décor, from "*The Sting*" to "*Paper Moon,*" the '40s and '50s had a special affectionate affinity for the manners and "look" of pre-Depression America. In the 1940s—the first decade in which all the major components of mass culture were up and running, even early television—the beloved focus of nostalgia were exactly the innocent aughts and teens of the early century, a taste ranging from *Meet Me in St. Louis*, a film made in 1944 about a fair held in 1904, to *Take Me Out to the Ball Game,* a musical made in 1948 about a song written in 1908. The '50s, in turn, brought about the revival of the jazz of the '20, with the essentially serious music of Joe Oliver and Jelly Roll Morton recast by middle-aged white men in straw boaters and striped jackets as something softer, called Dixieland. Perelman writing in the '40s and '50s about the teens and '20s, corresponds to the forty-year rule and took advantage of a common cultural preoccupation—one which rises from the truth that we have to cross into our own forties and fifties to at last become aware that the tastes of our adolescence were specific to our adolescences, not just a permanently shared obsession. Joni Mitchell may be for all time, but she belongs to 1971, though it takes until about 2010 to *feel* this. For Perelman, recognizing that the erotic frissons and mind-stirring adventures of his youth were now creaky and purely "period," had the same kind of fruitful comic shock and spoke to an audience who shared the memories.

*

"In so far as any writing can be said to be enjoyable—I categorically deny that it can—I find the new stuff of some slight absorbing interest while working on it," he further confided to Hadley, and this, coming from the saturnine Sid, is as close to an announcement of rapture-in-composition as one can ever hope to find from him. He wasn't wrong; of all the series he entertained in that period, from the end of the World War II to the arrival of rock music, The "Cloudland Revisited" pieces seem to this addicted Perelmanite to be much the best. One simple reason is that where the other ambitious projects—his *Acres and Pains* series about the remaking of a Bucks County farmhouse, or the many travel series that he undertook, often with the companionship of Al Hirschfeld, depend on the collision of the Perelman-of-the-page with conniving yokels or avaricious "natives," the "Cloudland Revisited" series depends on the less predictable collision of young Sid with old Sid. Young Sid, who is evoked in his wide-eyed absorption of the old movies—we see him attempting a makeshift dive in a homemade diving suit in Narragansett

Bay after viewing *Twenty Thousand Leagues Under the Sea*—is still infatuated with the stuff, while Older & Wiser Sid shakes his head retrospectively at the sheer intuitive surrealism of the story: "It more than equaled the all-time stowage record set by D.W. Griffith's *Intolerance*, managing to combine in one picture three unrelated plots—*Twenty Thousand Leagues*, *The Mysterious Island*, and *Five Weeks in a Balloon*—and a sanguinary tale of betrayal and murder in a native Indian state that must have fallen into the developing fluid by mistake."

And then "Cloudland" captures Perelman at his purest of heart. The facetious biographical note appended to one of the collections in which some of the "Cloudland" pieces were reprinted ends "He is twelve years old," and though this is obviously a po-faced statement of self-mockery, still it contains an element of truth. Sid *is* twelve years old, or at his best when he reinhabits his twelve-year-old self—when he is still in touch with the erotic-exotic fascinations of the old books and movies, and able to recreate, however mordantly, the sensitive and misunderstood boy who responded to them as much as the older man aghast at the quality of what he had to respond to. As old Sid narrates the movies, we sense both selves—he respects the spell cheap art cast on young Sid while breaking the spell for himself. Tales of infatuation and disillusion are braided together, in a kind of ecstatic counterpoint that leaves the series without the slightly arch and acidic tone that could creep into Perelman's parallel accounts of being swindled by Indonesian object-vendors or small-town plumbers.

*

Yet if the apparent object of these matchlessly entertaining pieces is the rueful memory of the seduction of a boy by false values, its real subject is the making of an American mind. That fault line on which his writing sits is a significant as any that occurs in American social history—the line between the Dave Brubeck and Ben Shahn sophistication of the late '50s and the Day-Glo colored pop art and rock music '60s. Perelman's attitudes in "Cloudland" are securely rooted in a set of "sophisticated" assumptions: Hollywood movies are uniformly terrible but have a kind of grotesque charm; the elaborate circumlocutions and self-consciousness of pop fiction—he was equally acute about Raymond Chandler's—are inherently ridiculous. Intelligence stood on the side of common sense and a stylish literate culture, and against the degradations of serious art into kitsch.

A scant ten years later, the bulwark had been broken, by Warhol and the Beatles at the higher end, and the kind of movies Perelman was mocking were not merely a source of archival responsibility, à la MoMA, but taken for granted as works of art worth placing alongside, and indeed above, Maugham or Galsworthy. The satiric tone that Perelman had mastered could suddenly seem merely supercilious—and indeed a superciliousness, barely containing the inevitable rage of the older writer at the newer world, infects his last pieces in the '60s and '70s.

Yet Perelman's unashamed infatuation with his own infant joys—what Nature was to Wordsworth, silent movies and pulp novels were to him—found its way fruitfully into the manner of the next generation, rather as the intuitive, "marginalized" fascination of the proto-Pop painters like Stuart Davis and Florine Stettheimer with American iconography became declaratively avant-garde in Pop art. Perelman made it possible for the first time to write a *papier collé* autobiography, one made of borrowed and assembled parts taken from the pop culture of one's time.

Though he would have been baffled—or bored—by the mechanized ironies of Pop art, Perelman was in many ways a Pop writer, given to distending the forms of old movies into new and still more hyperbolic shapes, as much as Claes Oldenburg making his monumental clothespins. It is hard to imagine the Tom Wolfe of the 1960s, for instance, with his deep dives, at once fascinated and horrified, into the mechanics of Phil Spector's wall of sound, or into the bosom-amplified go-go girls—writing that takes pop culture seriously and kids it at the same time—without the earlier example of Perelman. (That Wolfe both strenuously admired Perelman, and strenuously lectured him, for not being more of a "realist," i.e., more an overt moralist like Wolfe, is a sign of the Oedipal drama engendered.)

In another realm, Woody Allen's own early *New Yorker* pieces are almost comically detailed homages to the master. But at a level still deeper we feel Perelman's presence in the tension with which Allen's best movies hold in place a contempt for contemporary Hollywood alongside a reverence for the popular entertainment of Woody's own youth, as a reservoir of references and values. The movie *Radio Days*, for example, is a direct offspring of "Cloudland Revisited," in its bemused recounting of a retrospectively absurd cultural world that nonetheless still holds its fascination, as something that once seemed wholly realized and secure and has now entirely vanished. From Nicholson Baker to Michael Chabon, we routinely make novels and memoirs now out of our infatuation with pop entertainments past, winding our own experience around their cheap but unforgettable delights, making from the mass market entertainments of a commercial culture the private chapels of our private faiths. If this practice began anywhere, it began here.

Nor has the spell that Perelman cast on the movies that cast a spell on him lessened. On an August night in 2022, a long birthday evening walk took this writer and his family to the garden of the Museum of Modern Art for dinner. There, in a slightly separate but all too visible sector of the garden, MoMA was solemnly screening von Stroheim's *Foolish Wives*. The writer—this one—narrated it, almost shot by shot, to the astonished table, realizing that, never having seen it before, he recalled its sequences, and the sardonic sentences to go with them, almost perfectly from his fond recollection of Sid's fond recollection. Exactly as Sid had been beguiled and imprinted by silent movies, this writer had been beguiled and imprinted by Sid's sardonic ruminations on them. S. J. Perelman still can cast this secondary spell over his readers, who can no more escape his vision of how what he'd seen should be understood than he could escape the seductions of what he'd seen. "Cloudland Revisited" lives on in this way, as a palimpsest of American sensibilities, with new translucent layers added all the time: the follies of the 1920s made comic in the 1950s remain templates of our own reactions in the twenty-first century. The table laughs at long-ago vibrations of a matchless satiric mind. In this smaller way, great comic writing continues to make little earthquakes of its own.

CLOUDLAND REVISITED

Into Your Tent I'll Creep

I FIRST read *The Sheik*, by E. M. Hull, during the winter of 1922–23, standing up behind the counter of a curious cigar store of which I was the night clerk, though I preferred the loftier designation of relief manager. I was, at the time, a sophomore at Brown University and had no real need of the job, as I was wealthy beyond the dreams of avarice. I had taken it solely because my rooms were a rallying point for the *jeunesse dorée* and were so full of turmoil and inconsequential babble that I was driven to distraction. Like Stevenson's Prince Florizel of Bohemia, who retired into Soho to conduct his cigar divan under the pseudonym of Theophilus Godall, I wanted anonymity and a quiet nook for study and speculation. I got enough of all these to last a lifetime, and, by discreet pilfering, sufficient cigarettes to impair the wind of the entire student body. Five months after I joined the enterprise, it was stricken with bankruptcy, the medical name for mercantile atrophy. To claim that I was wholly responsible would be immodest. I did what I could, but the lion's share of the credit belonged to Mr. Saidy, who owned the store.

Mr. Saidy was a hyperthyroid Syrian leprechaun, and a man of extraordinarily diversified talents. He was an accomplished portrait painter in the academic tradition, and his bold, flashy canvases, some of which were stored in our stockroom, impressed me as being masterly. John Singer Sargent and Zuloaga, whom he plagiarized freely, might have felt otherwise, but since neither was in the habit of frequenting our stockroom, Mr. Saidy was pretty safe from recrimination. In addition to the painting, playing the zither, and carving peach pits into monkeys to grace his watch chain, he was an inventor. He had patented a pipe for feminine smokers that held cigarettes in a vertical position and a machine for extracting pebbles from gravel roofs. Saidy's entry into the tobacco business had been motivated by a romantic conviction that he could buck the United Cigar Store combine, using its own methods. We issued coupons with all purchases, redeemable, according to their guarantee, for hundreds of valuable premiums. I saw only four of them in my tenure—an electric iron, a catcher's mitt, a Scout knife, and one of those mechanical blackamoors of the period that operated on victrola turntables and danced a clog to "Bambalina" or "The Japanese Sandman." At first, I was uneasy lest some patron present a stack of coupons he had hoarded and demand one of the other premiums listed. There was no basis for my anxiety. Mr. Saidy's prices were higher than our competitors', so the customers stayed away by the thousands, and the infrequent few who blundered in spurned the certificates as if they were infected.

At any rate, it was in this pungent milieu that I made the acquaintance of the immortal Lady Diana Mayo and the Sheik Ahmed Ben Hassan, and when, after a lapse of twenty-five years, I sat down recently to renew it, I was heavy with nostalgia. A goodish amount of water had gone over the dam in the interim and I was not at all sure Miss Hull's febrile tale would pack its original wallop. I found that, contrariwise, the flavor had improved, like that of fine old port. There is nothing dated about the book; the bromides, in fact, have a creaminess, a velvet texture, I am certain they lacked a quarter of a century ago. Any connoisseur knows that a passage like "She hated him with all the strength of her proud, passionate nature" or "I didn't love you when I took you, I only wanted you to satisfy the beast in me" acquires a matchless bouquet from lying around the cellar of a second-hand bookshop. No slapdash artificial aging process can quite duplicate the tang. It must steep.

The opening paragraph of *The Sheik* is, possibly, the most superb example of direct plot exposition in the language. Instead of fussing over the table decorations and place cards, like so many novelists, the author whisks open the door of the range and serves the soufflé piping hot. In the very first line of the book, a disembodied voice asks someone named Lady Conway whether she is coming in to watch the dancing, and gets a tart reply: "I most decidedly am not. I thoroughly disapprove of the expedition of which this dance is the inauguration. I consider that even by contemplating such a tour alone into the desert with no chaperon or attendant of her own sex, with only native camel drivers and servants, Diana Mayo is behaving with a recklessness and impropriety that is calculated to cast a slur not only on her own reputation, but also on the prestige of her country. . . . It is the maddest piece of unprincipled folly I have ever heard of."

That, I submit, is literary honesty of a high order, to say nothing of a forensic style Cicero would have envied. It does not abuse the reader's patience with a complex psychological probe of Diana's youth, her awakening womanhood, her revolt against narrow social conventions. It tells him with a minimum of flubdub that a madcap miss is going to be loused up by Arabs and that there will be no exchanges or refunds. After making this speech, Lady Conway storms off. It transpires that she has been addressing two gentlemen on the veranda of the Biskra Hotel, an Englishman named Arbuthnot and an unnamed American, who take an equally dim view of Diana's temerity. Though both adore her, they are dismayed by her imprudence and heartlessness. "The coldest little fish in the world, without an idea in her head beyond sport and travel," as Arbuthnot subsequently describes her, has been reared by her brother, Sir Aubrey, a typical Du Maurier baronet, and obeys no bidding but her own whim. When Arbuthnot leaves to beg a dance of the minx, his rival speeds him with characteristic Yankee jocosity: "Run along, foolish moth, and get your poor little wings singed. When the cruel fair has done trampling on you I'll come right along and mop up the remains." I presume he punctuated this metaphoric nosegay with a jet of tobacco juice, slapped his thigh, and blew his nose into a capacious bandanna, but the text delicately makes no mention of it.

The singe, more of a second-degree burn, is administered in the garden, where Arbuthnot offers his hand to Diana, along with two memorable chestnuts to the effect that beauty like hers drives a man mad and that he won't always be a penniless subaltern. His avowals, however, go for nought, as does his plea that she abandon her foolhardy undertaking. She exhibits the same intransigence toward her brother the next evening, at the oasis to which he has escorted her. "I will do what I choose when and how I choose," she declares, turning up an already snub nose at his dark predictions, and, blithely promising to join him in New York, plunges into the trackless Sahara, accompanied only by a guide and several bodyguards. Had you or I written the story, our heroine would have cantered into Oran in due course with her nose peeling and a slight case of saddle gall. But sunburn alone does not create best-sellers, as Miss Hull well knew, and she has a bhoyo concealed in the dunes who is destined to put a crimp in Diana's plans, to phrase it very tactfully indeed.

For brevity's sake, we need not linger over the actual abduction of Diana by the Sheik; how her party is waylaid, how she is tempestuously swept onto his steed and spirited to his lair, must be tolerably familiar even to those too youthful to have seen it enacted on the screen by Agnes Ayres and Rudolph Valentino. The description of the desert corsair, though, as he takes inventory of his booty, attains a lyrical pitch current fiction has not surpassed: "It was the handsomest and cruelest face that she had ever seen. Her gaze was drawn instinctively to his. He was looking at her with fierce, burning eyes that swept her until she felt that the boyish clothes that covered her slender limbs were stripped from her, leaving the beautiful white body bare under his passionate stare." Under the circumstances, one cannot help feeling that her question, "Why have you brought me here?," betrays a hint of naïveté. The average man, faced with such a query, might have been taken unawares and replied weakly, "I forget," or "I guess I was overwhelmed by the sight of a pretty foot," but Ahmed's is no milksop answer: "*Bon Dieu!* Are you not woman enough to know?" This riposte so affected one spark I knew back in the early twenties that he used it exclusively thereafter in couch hammocks and canoes, but with what success is immaterial here. In the novel, at all events, the Arab chief, without further ado, works his sweet will of Diana, which explains in some measure why the book went into thirteen printings in eight months. I could be mistaken, of course; maybe it was only the sensuous lilt of the prose.

It may be asked, and reasonably, what the rest of the book deals with if such a ringing climax is reached on page 59. The story, simply, is one of adjustment; Ahmed Ben Hassan goes on working his sweet will of Diana with monotonous regularity, and she, in time, becomes reconciled to the idea. To be sure, she does not accept her martyrdom slavishly. She rages, threatens, implores, all to no purpose. Anguished, she demands why the Sheik has done this to her. "Because I wanted you," he returns coolly. "Because, one day in Biskra, four weeks ago, I saw you for a few moments, long enough to know that I wanted you. And what I want I take." All the scene needs to achieve perfection is a sardonic smile and a thin thread of smoke curling away from a monogrammed Turkish cigarette. These make their appearance in short order. Diana quaveringly asks when he will let her go. When he is tired of her, returns Ahmed with a sardonic smile, watching a thin thread of smoke curl away from a monogrammed Turkish cigarette. Small wonder every fiber of Diana's being cries out in protest.

"He is like a tiger," she murmurs deep into the cushions, with a shiver, "a graceful, cruel, merciless beast." She, in turn, reminds the Sheik of still another quadruped: "The easy swing of her boyish figure and the defiant carriage of her head reminded him of one of his own thoroughbred horses. . . . And as he broke them so would he break her." The connubial relationship between horse and tiger, while a trifle perplexing from the biological point of view, settles into a surprisingly domestic pattern. Yet instead of rolling with the punches, so to speak, Diana willfully upsets the applecart by running away. Ahmed overtakes her, and it is when she is being toted home, slung across his pommel like a sack of oats, that she experiences the great awakening: "Why did she not shrink from the pressure of his arm and the contact of his warm, strong body? . . . Quite suddenly she knew—knew that she loved him, that she had loved him for a long time, even when she thought she hated him and when she had fled from him. . . . He was a brute, but she loved him, loved him for his very brutality and superb animal strength."

Naturally, it would be infra dig for any woman, especially a member of the British peerage, to bluntly confess a *béguin* for an obscure tribesman. Hence, there ensues an interval in which Diana plays cat-and-mouse with the chieftain, instead of horse-and-tiger, and arouses his wrath by her ladylike reserve. "*Bon Dieu!* . . . Has the vile climate of your detestable country frozen you so thoroughly that nothing can melt you?" he mutters thickly, contemning even the weather in his scorn. "I am tired of holding an icicle in my arms." Eventually, though, his dear nearness, scorching kisses, and equally fiery rhetoric produce a thaw, and Diana favors him with a few caresses of signal puissance. Strange to say, their effect is not precisely what one would imagine: "'You go to my head, Diane,' he said with a laugh that was half anger, and shrugging his shoulders moved across the tent to the chest where the spare arms were kept, and unlocking it took out a revolver and began to clean it." Perhaps I was unduly stimulated, but after that torrid buildup, dilettantism with a pistol seemed no substitute for a volcano.

For all practical purposes, nevertheless, and halfway through her narrative, the author has proved to everyone's ennui that pride crumbles before primitive passion. Given another setting, the boy and girl could now trot around to the license bureau and legalize their union, but here, in addition to the lack of such facilities, there is still the embarrassing racial barrier confronting Diana. Bewitched as she is by her swain, she cannot quite blink at the fact that he is an Arab, a grubby little native by her social standards. To nullify this obstacle, the author puts some fairly ponderous machinery in motion. She introduces a lifelong chum of the Sheik, a novelist named the Vicomte Raoul de Saint Hubert, who also happens to be a crackajack surgeon. Then she causes Diana to be kidnaped by a rival sachem, from whom Ahmed rescues her, sustaining a grievous wound. As he hovers between life and death, watched over by the Vicomte and Diana, the gimmick is unveiled:

"'His hand is so big for an Arab's,' she said softly, like a thought spoken aloud unconsciously.

"'He is not an Arab,' replied Saint Hubert with sudden impatient vehemence, 'He is English.'" Yes, he continues, stunning Diana, if not the reader, his father is the Earl of Glencaryll. This news provokes a truly classic reaction from Diana: "Oh, now I know why that awful frown of Ahmed's has always seemed so familiar. Lord Glencaryll always frowns like that. It is the famous Caryll scowl." To soothe the literal-minded, there is a thirteen-page exegesis of the hero's background, complete with such reassuring details as a formal European education and a mother of noble Spanish birth. Diana doesn't really care, for she realizes that her woman's intuition, assisted by a bit of roughhouse from the Sheik, has guided her aright. When, on his recovery, he undergoes the mandatory change of heart and offers her freedom, the horse turns into a phoenix and rises reborn from the ashes: "She slid her arm up and around his neck, drawing his head down. 'I am not afraid,' she murmured slowly. 'I am not afraid of anything with your arms round me, my desert lover. Ahmed! Monseigneur!'"

If my examination of *The Sheik* did nothing else, it confirmed a suspicion I have been harboring for over two decades; namely, that the relief manager of a small cigar store in Providence about 1922 showed the most dubious literary taste of anyone I ever knew. To add to his other defects—he was shiftless, scheming, and transparently dishonest—he was an incorrigible romantic, the type of addlepate that, in later life, is addicted to rereading the books of his youth and whining over their shortcomings. Altogether, an unattractive figure and, I fear, a hopelessly bad lot. But then I suppose there's no point in being too tough on the boy. You can't judge people like him and Diana Mayo by ordinary standards. They're another breed of cat.

Tuberoses and Tigers

BACK in the summer of 1919, a fifteen-year-old youth at Riveride, Rhode Island, a watering place on the shores of upper Narragansett Bay, was a victim of a temporary but none the less powerful hallucination still referred to in southern New England as the "Riverside hallucination." For a space of three or four days, or until the effects of a novel called *Three Weeks*, by Elinor Glyn, had worn off, the boy believed himself to be a wealthy young Englishman named Paul Verdayne, who had been blasted by a searing love affair with a mysterious Russian noblewoman. His behavior during that period, while courteous and irreproachable to family and friends alike, was marked by fits of abstraction and a tendency to emit tragic, heartbroken sighs. When asked to sweep up the piazza, for instance, or bike over to the hardware store for a sheet of Tanglefoot, a shadow of pain would flit across his sensitive features and he would assent with a weary shrug. "Why not?" he would murmur, his lips curling in a bitter, mocking smile. "What else can life hold for me now?" Fortunately, his parents, who had seen him through a previous seizure in which he had identified himself with William S. Hart, were equipped to deal with his vagaries. They toned up his system with syrup of figs, burned his library card, and bought a second-hand accordion to distract him. Within a week, his distraction and that of the neighbors were so complete that the library card was hastily restored and the instrument disposed of—the latter no minor feat, as anyone knows who has ever tried to burn an accordion.

Not long ago, in a moment of nostalgia laced with masochism, it occurred to me to expose myself again to Miss Glyn's classic and see whether the years had diluted its potency. The only vivid recollection I preserved of the story was one of a sultry enchantress lolling on a tiger skin. I realized why the image had persisted when I ultimately tracked down a copy of the book. It was illustrated with scenes from the photoplay production Samuel Goldwyn gave it in 1924, and on the dust jacket, peering seductively at me across a snarling Indian man-eater, lay Aileen Pringle, mascaraed, braided, and palpitant with sex appeal. The very first page I sampled, before settling down to a leisurely feast, yielded a sweetmeat that corroborated my boyhood memory:

"A bright fire burnt in the grate, and some palest orchid-mauve silk curtains were drawn in the lady's room when Paul entered from the terrace. And loveliest sight of all, in front of the fire, stretched at full length was his tiger—and on him—also at full length—reclined the lady, garbed in some strange clinging garment of heavy purple *crêpe*, its hem embroidered with gold, one white arm resting on the beast's head, her back supported by a pile of the velvet cushions, and a heap of rarely bound books at her side, while between her lips was a rose not redder than they—an almost scarlet rose." It was very small wonder that when I originally read this passage, my breathing became shallow and I felt as if the Berea College choir were grouped in the base of my skull singing gems from Amy Woodford-Finden. Even the author seems to have had some fleeting compunction after writing it, for she went on hastily, "It was not what one would expect to find in a sedate Swiss hotel." If it thus affected Paul, you can guess what the impact was on Riverside, where our notion of barbaric splendor was a dish of fried eels.

Three Weeks touched off such a hullabaloo in England that, on its publication here, Miss Glyn wrote an exasperated preface for American readers, enjoining them to consider the spiritual rather than the fleshly aspects of her romance. "The minds of some human beings," she declared scornfully, "are as moles, grubbing in the earth for worms. . . . To such *Three Weeks* will be but a sensual record of passion." The real story, however, she explained, was the purifying effect upon a callow young Englishman of his gambol with a heroine whom Miss Glyn likened to a tiger (a simile she milked pretty exhaustively before the whistle blew) and described as "a great splendid nature, full of the passionate realization of primitive instincts, immensely cultivated, polished, blasé." She concluded her message with a request I am sure every novelist has longed to make at one time or another, and would if he had the courage: "And to all who read, I say—at least be just! and do not skip. No line is written without its having a bearing on the next, and in its small scope helping to make the presentment of these two human beings vivid and clear." I took the entreaty so much to heart that every last asterisk of *Three Weeks* was literally engraved on my brain, which, after two hundred and ninety pulsating pages, must have borne a striking resemblance to an old bath sponge peppered with buckshot.

The situation that obtains at the opening of Miss Glyn's fable, in all honesty, does not rank among the dizzier flights of the human imagination, but, in the vulgate of Vine Street, it's a springboard, and what the hell. Paul Verdayne, twenty-two years old, devastatingly handsome, and filthy with the stuff, has been dispatched by his elders on a tour of the Continent to cure his infatuation for a vicar's daughter. Nature, it appears, has been rather more bountiful to Paul's body and purse than to his intellect; above the ears, speaking bluntly, the boy is strictly tapioca. As the curtain rises on what is to be the most electrifying episode of his life, he is discovered moodily dining at a hotel in Lucerne and cursing his destiny. Suddenly, there comes to his nostrils the scent of tuberoses, and a lady materializes at the next table. At first, her exquisite beauty and sensuous elegance are lost on him; then, as she proceeds to sup on caviar, a blue trout, *selle d'agneau au lait*, a nectarine, and Imperial Tokay, he perceives he is face to face with a thoroughbred, and the old familiar mixture of fire and ice begins stirring in his veins. Without any sign that she has noticed his presence, she glides out, overwhelming the young man with her figure: "'She must have the smallest possible bones,' Paul said to himself, 'because it looks all curvy and soft, and yet she is as slender as a gazelle.'" On a diet like the foregoing, I wouldn't give odds the lady would stay gazelle-slender perpetually, but perhaps her metabolism was as unusual as her charm. In any case, there is, as everyone is aware, a standard procedure for those smitten by mysterious sirens smelling of tuberoses; namely, to smoke a cigar pensively on the terrace, soothe one's fevered senses, and await developments. Paul faithfully adheres to the convention, and at length the lady, presumably having nullified gastritis with a fast Pepto-Bismol, slithers out onto her balcony and casts him a languishing glance. From that point on, it is *sauve-qui-peut* and prudent readers will do well to hold *Three Weeks* at arm's length, unless they want to be cut by flying adjectives.

In the ensuing forty-eight hours, Mme. Zalenska, as Paul ascertains her name to be from the register, plays a hole-and-corner game with her caballero, ogling him from behind beech trees, undulating past him in hotel corridors, and generally raising the deuce with his aplomb. Finally, when she has reduced him to the consistency of jellied consommé, she summons him to her suite for a short midnight powwow. The décor is properly titillating and, inevitably, includes Miss Glyn's favorite carnivore: "The lights were low and shaded, and a great couch filled one side of the room beyond the fireplace. Such a couch! covered with a tiger skin and piled with pillows, all shades of rich purple velvet and silk, embroidered with silver and gold—unlike any pillows he had ever seen before, even to their shapes." Paul, in his pitiable innocence, assumes he has been called to render some neighborly service, like installing a new Welsbach mantle or cobbling Zalenska's shoes. Actually, she wishes to warn him how lethal she is:

"'Look at me,' she said, and she bent forward over him—a gliding feline movement infinitely sinuous and attractive. . . . Her eyes in their narrowed lids gleamed at him, seeming to penetrate into his very soul. . . . Suddenly she sprang up, one of those fine movements of hers, full of cat-like grace. 'Paul,' she said . . . and she spoke rather fast. 'You are so young, so young—and I shall hurt you—probably. Won't you go now—while there is yet time? Away from Lucerne, back to Paris—even back to England. Anywhere away from me.'" Had Paul, at this juncture, slipped into his reefer and whistled for a fiacre, it might have saved both him and me considerable anguish, but Miss Glyn's royalties certainly would have been stricken with anemia. He therefore gallantly confides his heart into the lady's custody, snatches up an armful of tube-roses, and retires to the terrace to stride up and down until dawn, soothing his fevered senses. This is technically known in Publishers' Row as a tease play or the punch retarded, a stratagem designed to keep the savages guessing.

In a brief pastoral interlude next day, idling about the lake in a luxurious motor launch heaped with even stranger pillows and dialogue, Mme. Zalenska's mood is alternately maternal and bombastic. "I wish to be foolish today, Paul," she says (a program she achieves with notable success), "and see your eyes dance, and watch the light on your curls." His ardor becomes well-nigh unendurable when, before teatime, she bends over him with the tantalizing comment "Great blue eyes! So pretty, so pretty!," and he hoarsely begs her for instruction in the art of love. Her orotund answer sets the placid bosom of the lake rippling: "Yes, I will teach you! Teach you a number of things. Together we will put on the hat of darkness and go down into Hades. We shall taste the apples of the Hesperides—we will rob Mercure of his sandals—and Gyges of his ring." Just as the steam is bubbling in Paul's gauges, however, Mme. Zalenska laughingly twists out of his grasp, and another sequence ends with the poor *schlemiel* patrolling his beat on the terrace. Whatever deficiencies of logic the author may display on occasion, she surely cannot be accused of hurrying her climax.

The spark that ignites the tinder, oddly enough, is a gift Paul purchases for his affinity—one of those characteristic souvenirs that litter sedate Swiss hotels, a tiger skin. "It was not even dear as tigers go, and his parents had given him ample money for any follies." Sprawled out on it, strange greenish flames radiating from her pupils, Mme. Zalenska goads the boy to the brink of neurasthenia by withholding the tuition she promised and proposing in its stead a literary debauch. "'Paul,' she cooed plaintively, 'tomorrow I shall be reasonable again, perhaps, and human, but today I am capricious and wayward, and mustn't be teased. I want to read about Cupid and Psyche from this wonderful *Golden Ass* of Apuleius—just a simple tale for a wet day—and you and—me!'" By then, though, the lad in his own stumble-foot fashion has evolved a more piquant formula for passing a rainy day, and, with a prodigious amount of whinnying, purring, gurgling, and squealing, the education of Paul Verdayne swings into its initial phase.

How high a voltage the protagonists generate in the two remaining weeks of their affair, I cannot state with precision; the dial on my galvanometer burst shortly afterward, during a scene where they are shown cradled in a hotel on the Bürgenstock, exchanging baby talk and feeding each other great, luscious red strawberries. At Venice, to which they migrate for no stringent reason except that the author wanted to ring in a vignette of Mme. Zalenska biting Paul's ear lobes in a gondola, there is an account of their pleasure dome that deserves attention:

"The whole place had been converted into a bower of roses. The walls were entirely covered with them. A great couch of deepest red ones was at one side, fixed in such masses as to be quite resisting and firm. From the roof chains of roses hung, concealing small lights—while from above the screen of lilac-bushes in full bloom the moon in all her glory mingled with the rose-shaded lamps and cast a glamour and unreality over the whole. . . . The dinner was laid on a table in the center, and the table was covered with tuberoses and stephanotis, surrounding the cupid fountain of perfume."

And now the plot, hitherto snowed under by suchlike verdant *Katzenjammer*, refuses any longer to be denied. Awakening one noonday from his finals, which he has evidently passed *summa cum laude*, Paul finds a farewell note from his coach, setting forth that they must part forever, inasmuch as sinister forces in her background endanger both their lives. There have been sketchy intimations earlier that Mme. Zalenska is some sort of empress on a toot, or at least a margravine, and Paul has observed several dubious Muscovites tailing them around St. Mark's but, in his exaltation, has dismissed them as phantoms induced by over-work. The realization that he is henceforth cut off from postgrad-uate study exerts its traditional effect, and he goes down like a poled ox. By the time Sir Charles, his father, has arrived bearing cold compresses and beef tea, Paul lies between life and death, madly raving with brain fever. His convalescence, of course, fol-lows the mandatory pattern—the Adriatic cruise aboard a conve-nient yacht, the Byronic soliloquies in the moonlight, and, back in England, the solitary rambles on the moors with the devoted rough-coated terrier. As time assuages his grief, a new Paul re-enters British society, older, fluent, worldly-wise. He prepares to stand for Parliament, scores a brilliant social success: "He began to be known as someone worth listening to by men, and women hung on his words. . . . And then his complete indifference to them piqued and allured them still more. Always polite and chivalrous, but as aloof as a mountain top." I don't want to sound vindictive, but can you imagine asking a man like that to scoot over to the hardware store for ten cents' worth of fly rolls? That's the kind of thing I was up against on Narragansett Bay thirty years ago.

The rest of *Three Weeks* is soon told, although not soon enough, frankly, by Miss Glyn, who consumes fifty marshmallow-filled pages to accomplish what she might have in two. After an endless amount of palaver, she discloses that Paul's and Zalenska's seminar has resulted in a bonny little cub and that, for all their pledges of devotion, the lovers are never reunited. The latter oversight is excused by as nimble a washup as you will find anywhere in the post-Victorian novel: "Everyone knows the story which at the time convulsed Europe. How a certain evil-living King, after a wild orgie of mad drunkenness, rode out with two boon companions to the villa of his Queen, and there, forcing an entrance, ran a dagger through her heart before her faithful servants could protect her. And most people were glad, too, that this brute paid the penalty of his crime by his own death—his worthless life choked out of him by the Queen's devoted Kalmuck groom." This salubrious housecleaning elevates the tot to the throne, and as the book ends, Paul kneels in the royal chapel before the boy, quivering with paternal pride and chauvinism: "The tiny upright figure in its blue velvet suit, heavily trimmed with sable, standing there proudly. A fair, rosy-cheeked, golden-haired English child . . . And as he gazed at his little son, while the organ pealed out a Te Deum and the sweet choir sang, a great rush of tenderness filled Paul's heart, and melted forever the icebergs of grief and pain."

A few hours after finishing *Three Weeks*, there came to me out of the blue a superb concept for a romantic novel, upon which I have been laboring like a demon ever since. In essence, it is the story of an incredibly handsome and wealthy youth of forty-four whose wife and children, dismayed by his infatuation for servant-girl literature, pack him off to Switzerland. There he meets and falls in love with a ravishing twenty-three-year-old girl, half tigress and half publisher. The tigress in her fascinates him at the same time that the publisher revolts him, and out of this ambivalence, so to speak, grows the conflict. . . . But why am I telling you all this? I can see you're really not listening.

How Ruritanian Can You Get?

I TRUST I may be spared the accusation of being an old fogy, but prices these days are really unconscionable. As recently as 1918, it was possible for a housewife in Providence, where I grew up, to march into a store with a five-cent piece, purchase a firkin of cocoa butter, a good second-hand copy of Bowditch, a hundredweight of quahogs, a shagreen spectacle case, and sufficient nainsook for a corset cover, and emerge with enough left over to buy a balcony admission to *The Masquerader*, with Guy Bates Post, and a box of maxixe cherries. What the foregoing would cost her today I shudder to think; one fairly affluent Rhode Islander I met last summer confessed to me that he simply could not afford a pat of cocoa butter for his nose, and as for corset covers, his wife just threw up her hands. Along with the necessities of life, labor in the early twenties was unbelievably abundant and cheap. Imagine, for example, being able to hire the recording secretary of the Classical High School debating society—a man whose mordant irony reminded his auditors of Disraeli and Brann the Iconoclast, although he had scarcely turned sixteen—to sift your ashes and beat your carpets at thirty cents an hour. Even I find it almost too fantastic to credit, and, mind you, I *was* the recording secretary.

It was while sifting and beating about the home of a Providence chatelaine one spring afternoon that I came into possession of a book that was to exert a powerful influence on me for a long time to come. In a totally inexplicable burst of generosity, my employer, an odious Gorgon in brown bombazine, presented me with an armload of novels that had been moldering in her storeroom more than a decade. Among them, I recall, were such mellow favorites as *V.V.'s Eyes*, by Henry Sydnor Harrison; *Satan Sanderson* and *A Furnace of Earth*, by Hallie Erminie Rives; William J. Locke's *The Beloved Vagabond*; *The Goose Girl*, by Harold MacGrath; and *Graustark*, George Barr McCutcheon's best-seller published at the turn of the century. Curled up in my den on a mound of pillows covered with the flags of all nations, I consumed the lot in a single evening, buffeted by emotional typhoons so tempestuous that the family twice broke down the door to discover the cause of my spectacular groans and sighs. The one that gave me the most lasting belt was *Graustark*. Not since Janvier's masterly *In the Sargasso Sea*, a thrilling saga of the adventures of two boys mired in the North Atlantic kelp, had I read a story charged with such arresting characters and locales, such bravado and rollicking high humor. As I sped with Grenfall Lorry from our Western plains to the crags of Edelweiss in his mad pursuit of the beauteous Miss Guggenslocker, it seemed to me that for sheer plot invention and felicity of phrase McCutcheon must forever dwarf any other novelist in the language. For at least a fortnight afterward, I patterned myself on his insouciant hero, spouting jaunty witticisms like "You tell 'em, goldfish, you've been around the globe" and behaving with a nervous hilarity that sent acquaintances scuttling around corners at my approach.

Several months back, I was sequestered over a rainy weekend in a cottage at Martha's Vineyard whose resources consisted of a crokinole board and half a dozen romances of the vintage of those mentioned above. By an electrifying coincidence, the first one I cracked turned out to be *Graustark*. Our reunion, like most, left something to be desired. I do not think I had changed particularly; perhaps my reflexes were a little less elastic, so I often had to backtrack forty or fifty pages to pick up the thread, and occasionally I fell into a light reverie between chapters, but in the main my mind had lost none of its vacuity and was still as supple as a moist gingersnap. *Graustark*, on the other hand, had altered almost beyond recognition. During the twenty-eight intervening years, it was apparent, some poltergeist had sneaked in and curdled the motivation, converted the hero into an insufferable jackanapes, drawn mustaches on the ladies of the piece, and generally sprinkled sneeze powder over the derring-do. Of course, mine was a purely personal reaction, and the average bobby-soxer reading it for the first time would doubtless disagree, but, as they say on the outer boulevards, *chacun à son* goo.

The principals of *Graustark*—a wealthy young American sportsman named Grenfall Lorry and a fair blue-blood traveling, under the laborious incognito of Sophia Guggenslocker, with her aunt and uncle—meet at the outset in this country aboard a transcontinental express, a setting subsequently much favored by the Messrs. Ambler, Greene, and Hitchcock in their entertainments. Apart from this footling resemblance, though, McCutcheon lacks any visible kinship with those masters of suspense; for instance, he jealously withholds the secret of his heroine's identity for a hundred and fifty-five glutinous pages, long past the point where you care whether she is the Princess Yetive of Graustark or Hop-o'-My-Thumb. Lorry is the type of popinjay who was ubiquitous in the novels of the nineteen-hundreds but has largely disappeared from current fiction. He has been everywhere, done everything; he has an income "that had withstood both the Maison Dorée and a dahabeah on the Nile," and, as the author explains in as natty a syllepsis as you will find in a month's hard search through Fowler, "he had fished through Norway and hunted in India, and shot everything from grouse on the Scottish moors to the rapids above Assouan." He is, in fine, a pretty speedy customer, and the photographs of him in the text, taken from the play version, confirm it. Even if his toupee is askew and his pepper-and-salt trousers are so baggy in the seat as to suggest that he is concealing a brace of grouse, Grenfall Lorry is a cove to be reckoned with.

In accordance with the usual ground rules, Miss Guggenslocker's dimples effectively snare Lorry as their train chuffs out of Denver, and he sets himself to further their acquaintance through a number of ruses too roguish to be exhumed. That she is not wholly oblivious is evidenced as he vaults aboard the carriage after a brief stop: "There was an expression of anxiety in her eyes as he looked up into them, followed instantly by one of relief. . . . She had seen him swing upon the moving steps and had feared for his safety—had shown in her glorious face that she was glad he did not fall beneath the wheels." This display of feeling, while not quite tantamount to an invitation to creep into her sleeping bag, nevertheless heartens Lorry and he perseveres. His opportunity comes when the two of them, through an elephantine convolution of the plot, are temporarily marooned in a mining town in the Alleghenies. Frenziedly careering through mountain passes in an ancient stage, Lorry assists the lady in rejoining the train, learns she is a Graustarkian, and, in the course of their intimacy, revs himself up to a rather alarming pitch of emotion: "Her sweet voice went tingling to his toes with every word she uttered. He was in a daze, out of which sung the mad wish that he might clasp her in his arms, kiss her, and then go tumbling down the mountain." Safe again on the flier, Miss Guggenslocker commends him to her party for his gallantry but in the next breath dashes his hopes; she is about to sail for home on the *Kaiser Wilhelm der Grosse*. They share an idyllic afternoon of sightseeing in Washington (during which they glimpse President Cleveland taking a constitutional, a sight that mysteriously evokes a ringing eulogy on our democratic process) and part with Lorry's fierce assurance that he will some-day follow her to Graustark—possibly the most paltry bon-voyage gift ever tendered a girl in the history of the American novel.

For the sake of brevity, a virtue McCutcheon cannot be said to have held in idolatry, we may dust lightly over Lorry's *Sturm und Drang* in the months that follow, his departure for Graustark, and his arrival in Edelweiss, the capital of that country, in the company of Harry Anguish, an ex-Harvard classmate as painfully blithe as himself. The profundity and broad social tolerance of the latter can be gauged from his reactions as they near Edelweiss, the capital: "I'll be glad when we can step into a decent hotel, have a rub, and feel like white men once more. I am beginning to feel like those dirty Slavs and Huns we saw 'way back there." The search for Lorry's inamorata leads them to the chief of police, a Baron Dangloss, whose name appears to be a suspicious hybrid of Danglers, in *The Count of Monte Cristo*, and Pangloss, the phi-losopher of *Candide*, though he has none of the savor of either. Dangloss foxily pretends not to know who Miss Guggenslocker is, and Lorry is on the verge of defenestrating himself when he spies her in a royal carriage guarded by footmen and outriders. To his dismay, she drives on with only the most casual sign of recognition, but inside the hour a groom arrives with a note bidding him to call on her the next day. As Lorry, still without any suspicion of her actual identity, ponders these baffling developments, his colleague offers a deduction right out of 221B Baker Street. "I'll tell you what I've worked out during the past two minutes," he announces portentously. "Her name is no more Guggenslocker than mine is. She and the uncle used that name as a blind." It is plain as day that there are no flies on Harry Anguish. Those little black specks you see are merely vertigo.

Before the scheduled meeting can take place, the plot suddenly puts forth a series of tendrils and strangles the reader like a tropical liana. Strolling under the castle walls that evening, Lorry and Anguish overhear a design to abduct Princess Yetive. Conveniently for them, the conspirators couch it in a language they can grasp: "We must be careful to speak only in English. There are not twenty people in Edelweiss who understand it, but the night has ears." Ensues a sequence bristling with muffled oaths, judo, and chloroform, at the end of which Lorry bilks the kidnapers and discovers Miss Guggenslocker to be the Princess Yetive. What with the impact of this thunderbolt and a felonious blow on the sconce, he falls senseless, and spends the following chapter being nursed back to health by his royal sweetheart. Instead of their developing the rapport one would normally expect, though, it now transpires that Yetive's throne stands between the lovers; their dialogue resounds with echoing periods like "I find a princess and lose a woman!" and "The walls which surround the heart of a princess are black and grim, impenetrable when she defends it, my boasting American." There is, in addition, a whole labyrinthine complex of political reasons why Graustark girl and Melican boy may not fuse at the moment, and, reining his narrative back on its haunches, McCutcheon proceeds to catalogue them with all the exhaustive detail of a Gibbon or a Macaulay.

Boiled down to their marrow, it seems that Graustark, in consequence of a disastrous war with Axphain, a bordering state, owes its neighbors twenty-five million gavvos it cannot pay. Bankruptcy and dishonor face the nation, and Yetive, who is *de-facto* ruler, is nearly beside herself with anxiety. "Her Royal Highness," Lorry is told by Count Halfont, her uncle, "spent the evening with the ministers of finance and war, and her poor head, I doubt not, is racking from the effects of the consultation. These are weighty matters for a girl to have on her hands." Eventually, Yetive's head stops racking, and she agrees to marry Lorenz of Axphain to lift the mortgage, notwithstanding Lorry's reproaches and tantrums. The second the betrothal is announced, a chain of fictional firecrackers begins exploding. Lorenz of Axphain, a debauchee and wastrel, utters a coarse jape about Yetive in a saloon, sustains a haymaker from Lorry, and demands satisfaction under the code. Just before the duel, he is found murdered; Lorry is accused, on circumstantial evidence, and is flung into poky. His release is effected by a bosomy hussar with a piping voice and a strangely reminiscent perfume, who persists in shielding her face as they flee in a carriage. Lorry, hardly what might be called the intuitive sort, at last surrenders to curiosity and insists on seeing his benefactor's features: "Below the arm that hid the eyes and nose he saw parted lips and a beardless, dainty chin; above, long, dark tresses strayed in condemning confusion. The breast beneath the blue coat heaved convulsively." In the next moment, the soldier melts into the fugitive's arms and the prose into nougat: "The lithe form quivered and then became motionless in the fierce, straining embrace; the head dropped upon his shoulder, his hot lips caressing the burning face and pouring wild, incoherent words into the little ears. 'You! You!' he cried, mad with joy. 'Oh, this is Heaven itself! My brave darling! Mine forever—mine forever! You shall never leave me now! Drive on! Drive on!' he shouted to the men outside, drunk with happiness. 'We'll make this journey endless. I know you love me now—I know it! God, I shall die with joy!'" The degree of fever this passage induced in me at sixteen was so intense that steam issued from my ears and I repeatedly had to sluice myself down with ice water. At forty-four, while it is true my breathing grew increasingly stertorous, it was marked by a rhythmical whistling sound, and had a cigarette not fallen on my chest in the nick of time, I would still be hibernating on Martha's Vineyard, and nobody the wiser.

It would be permissible to suppose that Lorry and his sugarplum are now ready for the orange blossoms and flat silver, but anyone who did so would indulge in wishful thinking. Yetive, stashing her beau at a monastery until he cools off officially and personally, returns to confront problems of state. The enraged Axphainians insist on Harry Anguish's being held as a hostage, and finally propose to remit the national tribute if Lorry is captured and executed. Meanwhile, as if to further befog his lens, the author whips in yet another complication, a satanic toad of a monarch named Gabriel of Dawsbergen, likewise hungry for Yetive and prepared to square the debt in exchange for her hand. The whole fragrant chowder comes to a boil when Lorry steals back to visit the Princess, is surprised in her boudoir by the aforementioned Gabriel, and is blackmailed into giving himself up. Ultimately, in a climactic scene that travels with the speed of library paste, Gabriel is publicly unmasked by Anguish as both the assassin of Lorenz and the engineer of the scheme to snatch Yetive, and Axphain generously agrees to laugh off the horrid old indemnity that has been animating the plot. Amid popular rejoicing, Yetive persuades her ministers to accept Lorry as prince consort, Anguish and a countess he has been spoony on pair off, and as the book slips from one's nerveless fingers the foursome leaves in a shower of ennui for Washington, D.C.

I forget exactly what Eastern religion it is, whether Buddhism or Taoism, that holds that life is entirely a series of repetitions and that everything we experience has happened before. If I ever doubted it, it was proved overpoweringly that afternoon on the Vineyard. Within ten minutes after I finished rereading *Graustark*, a sensitive young kid on the order of Barbara LaMarr knocked timidly on the door and offered to sift my ashes or beat the carpets for a simply laughable fee. Inasmuch as I was only a house guest, I had no need of her services, but I presented her with a novel that had been moldering on my chest all day, and you've never seen anyone so bowled over. Poor thing broke down, and if I hadn't caught her in time, I believe she would have fainted; upon my soul I do. I was pretty moved myself—one of those cases where the gift enriches the giver as well, I guess. Oh, pshaw, you mustn't mind my running on. I act this way every time I get near one of those mythical kingdoms.

Sodom in the Suburbs

THE CLOSEST I ever came to an orgy, aside from the occasion in Montparnasse twenty years ago when I smoked a cigarette purported to contain hashish and fainted dead away after two puffs, was at a student dance at Brown around 1922. I did not suspect it was an orgy until three days later; in fact, at the time it seemed to me decorous to the point of torpor and fully consonant with the high principles of the Brown Christian Association, under whose auspices it was held. Attired in a greenish Norfolk jacket and scuffing the massive bluchers with perforated toe caps and brass eyelets considered *de rigueur* in that period, I spent the evening buffeting about in the stag line, prayerfully beseeching the underclassmen I knew for permission to cut in on their women and tread a few measures of the Camel Walk. At frequent intervals, noisily advertising an overpowering thirst, I retired to a cloakroom with several other blades and choked down a minute quantity of gin, warmed to body heat, from a pocket flask. Altogether, it was a strikingly commonplace experience, and I got to bed without contusions and stayed there peaceably riffling through *Jurgen* and humming snatches of "Avalon."

The following Sunday, I learned, to my astonishment, that I had been involved in a momentous debauch; the campus reeked of a scandal so sulphurous that it hung over our beanies like a nimbus for the rest of the academic year. In blazing scareheads, the Hearst *Boston American* tore the veil from the excesses tolerated at Brown University dances. At these hops, it thundered, were displayed a depravity and libertinism that would have sickened Petronius and made Messalina hang her head in shame. It portrayed girls educated at the best finishing schools, crazed with alcohol and inflamed by ragtime, oscillating cheek to cheek with young ne'er-do-wells in raccoon coats and derbies. Keyed up by savage jungle rhythms, the *abandonnés* would then reel out to roadsters parked on Waterman Street, where frat pins were traded for kisses under cover of darkness. Worst of all, and indicative of the depths to which the Jazz Age had reduced American womanhood, was the unwritten law that each girl must check her corset before the saturnalia. Painting a picture that combined the more succulent aspects of the Quatz' Arts Ball and a German officers' revel in occupied Belgium—two types of wassail long cherished by Hearst feature writers—the writer put all his metaphors in one basket and called upon outraged society to apply the brakes, hold its horses, and retrieve errant youth from under the wheels of the juggernaut. It was a daisy, and whoever did the pen drawings that enhanced it had given a lot of thought to the female bust.

I was poignantly reminded of that epoch and its turbulent escapades the other afternoon as I sat puffing a meerschaum and turning the leaves of a novel called *Flaming Youth*, which attained an immense vogue about that time not only with the general public but with the owner of the meerschaum. The book was hailed by press and pulpit as a blistering, veracious study of the moral chaos prevalent in the upper brackets, and it was popularly believed

that its author, ostensibly a physician writing under the pseudonym of Warner Fabian, was, in reality, a top-drawer novelist. If
he was, he successfully managed to conceal it; his style, at once
flamboyant, euphuistic, and turgid, suggested nothing quite so
much as melted marzipan. Fabian was plainly determined to leave
no scintilla of doubt that he was a neophyte, for he wrote a windy
foreword affirming it, the final segment of which seems to me to
prove his claim incontestably: "To the woman of the period thus
set forth, restless, seductive, greedy, discontented, craving sensation, unrestrained, a little morbid, uneducated, sybaritic, following blind instincts and perverse fancies, slack of mind as she is
trim of body, neurotic and vigorous, a worshiper of tinseled gods
at perfumed altars, fit mate for the hurried, reckless, and cynical
man of the age, predestined mother of—what manner of being?:
To Her I dedicate this study of herself." I don't know why, but I
got the feeling from the foregoing that the doctor was a precise
and bloodless little creep with a goatee I would dearly love to
tweak. I could just see him whipping to his feet at a panel of nose
specialists, removing his pince-nez with maddening deliberation,
and beginning, "With the permission of the chair, I should like to
amplify Dr. Westerphal's masterly orientation of the Eustachian
tubes."

The fictional family chosen by the author to typify the deca-
dence of the twenties is named Fentriss, resident in a well-to-do
Westchester or Long Island suburb called Dorrisdale. Stripped of
its gingerbread, the story concerns itself with the amours of the
three Fentriss daughters, Constance, Dee, and Pat, whose adolescence has been colored by their mother's reckless hedonism.
She, while delectable, sounds from Fabian's thumbnail description very much like an early Cubist portrait by Picasso: "She was

a golden-brown, strong, delicately rounded woman, glowing with an effect of triumphant and imperishable youth. Not one of her features but was faulty by strict artistic tenets; even the lustrous eyes were set at slightly different levels." Mona Fentriss's life of self-indulgence has done more than throw her features out of whack; in the opening stanza, we see her being told by her physician and devoted admirer, Dr. Robert Osterhout, that there are fairies at the bottom of her aorta and that her days are numbered. Osterhout is a gruff, lovable character in the best medico-literary tradition: "Like a bear's, his exterior was rough, shaggy, and seemed not to fit him well. His face was irregularly square, homely, thoughtful, and humorous." Ever the heedless pagan, Mona turns a deaf ear to the voice of doom and, over the single shakerful of cocktails the doctor has restricted her to daily, confesses no remorse for her numerous extramarital affairs. Her husband, she confides, is equally unconcerned at her peccadilloes ("They say he's got a Floozie now, tucked away in a cozy corner somewhere"), and it is a lead-pipe cinch that, given this profligate environment and dubious heredity, the Fentriss girls are going to cut some pretty spectacular didos once the saxophones start sobbing.

We get our first peep at the dissipation extant in the household at a party thrown by Mona shortly afterward and characterized as follows: "The party was a Bingo. . . . Lovely, flushed, youthful, regnant in her own special queendom, Mona Fentriss sat in the midst of a circle of the older men, bandying stories with them in voices which were discreetly lowered when any of the youngsters drew near. It was the top of the time." Pat, the youngest daughter, has been considered too young to attend, but she abstracts a dinner dress from one of her sisters and eavesdrops in the shrubbery.

A furious crap game rages in the breakfast nook, furtive giggles emanate from parked cars, and, in the conservatory, Pat overhears her mother holding an equivocal duologue with Sidney Rathbone, an elderly but distinguished Baltimorean of nearly forty. A moment later, a glass of home brew is rudely forced to Pat's lips; as she recoils from the searing liquid, she is kissed violently and an insinuating voice pleads in her ear, "Come on, sweetie! We'll take a fifty-mile-an-hour dip into the landscape. The little boat [automobile, in the argot of '22] can go some." Much to Pat's discomfiture, however, her mother intercedes, routs the befuddled Princetonian besieging her daughter, and packs her off to bed. But the damage has been done, and, as Fabian darkly observes, tucking back his sleeves and preparing to fold a spoonful of cantharides into his already piquant meringue, that first smacker is the one a girl never forgets.

The narrative jogs along uneventfully for a spell, enlivened by a couple of minor scandals: Mrs. Fentriss shacks up briefly at a hotel called the Marcus Groot, in Trenton, with the aforesaid Sidney Rathbone, and Constance, the eldest daughter, underestimates her resistance to Bacardi, passes out in her cavalier's room, and is forced to still gossiping tongues by marrying him. A quick time lapse now enables the author to dispose of the exuberant Mrs. Fentriss and dress the stage for the entrance of the hero, Cary Scott, a former flame of hers encountered on a trip abroad. The description of Scott, clad in a sealskin coat and astrakhan cap, sufficiently explains why he sets the Fentriss girls by the ears: "No woman would have called him handsome. His features were too irregular, and the finely modeled forehead was scarred vertically with a savagely deep V which mercifully lost itself in the clustering hair, a testimony to active war service. There was confident distinction in his bearing, and an atmosphere of quiet and somewhat ironic worldliness in voice and manner. He looked to be a man who had experimented much with life in its larger meaning and found it amusing but perhaps not fulfilling." Nor does he become less glamorous when he admits, in the cultivated accents of one more at home in French than in his native tongue, that he has lived much out of the world: "The East; wild parts of Hindustan and northern China; and then the South Seas. I have a boy's passion for travel." This suave customer, understandably, makes the youths at the Dorrisdale country club seem pretty loutish to radiant, eighteen-year-old Pat, and she falls headlong. He reciprocates in flippant, half-serious fashion, regarding her as merely another spoiled flapper; besides, like all distinguished men of the world with deep Vs, he is chained to an impossible wife in Europe, and even the most beef-witted reader must appreciate what plot convulsions are required to reconcile such opposites.

An episode of mixed nude bathing next ensues to blueprint the élan of the younger set, in the course of which the guests, emboldened by draughts of a potation called a "submarine cocktail," cavort about a pool in a thunderstorm pinching each other. In consequence, Dee, the second Fentriss girl, weds a rotter; Cary Scott goes back to Paris; and Pat is sent away to school. When Cary sees her on his return, she has burgeoned into what he terms a "*petite gamine*," a phrase she does not understand; evidently she has been attending some technical school, like the Delehanty Institute. "You know what a gamin is?" he inquires. "*Gamine* is the feminine. But there's a suggestion in it of something more delicate and fetching; of verve, of—of *diablerie*." Leave it to those expatriates to explain one French word with another; he might at least have gone on to tell her that *diablerie* was derived from the game of diavolo, just making its appearance in the smarter salons of the Faubourg St. Honoré. Anyhow, he takes her to a concert, where Tchaikovsky's Fifth Symphony makes them kin-spirits, and, swept away by the bassoons, kisses her. Almost instantly, though, he feels the lash of conscience and excoriates himself in a noteworthy soliloquy: "It was incredible; it was shameful; it was damnable; but this child, this *petite gamine*, this reckless, careless, ignorant, swift-witted, unprincipled, selfish, vain, lovable, impetuous, bewildering, seductive, half-formed girl had taken his heart in her two strong, shapely woman-hands, and claimed it away from him—for what? A toy? A keepsake? A treasure? What future was there for this abrupt and blind encounter of his manhood and her womanhood?" Follows a thirty-one-page renunciation jam-packed with rough tenderness, eyes shadowed with pain, and germane claptrap, and Cary vamooses to California. There was one thing you could be reasonably sure of in any novel published between 1915 and 1925: the minute the protagonists got within biting distance of each other, one of them was fated to board a boat or choo-choo within seventy-two hours.

As might be anticipated, Pat thereupon reacts in accordance with the protocol governing the broken-hearted and plunges into a mad round of pleasure, careering around the countryside at 40 m.p.h. in sleek Marmon runabouts, ingesting oceans of hooch, and inhaling straw-tipped Melachrinos. When Cary, despite himself, is drawn back to her, he finds her more provocative than ever, a disturbing amalgam of elf, kitten, and bacchante: "She shook the gleamy mist of her hair about her face, gave a gnomish twist to body and neck, and peered sidelong at him from out the tangle." His punctilio holds fast until someone next door idly starts plucking a fiddle, and then hell breaks loose again: "The long, thrilling, haunted wind-borne prayer of the violin penetrated the innermost fiber of her, mingling there with the passionate sense of his nearness, swaying her to undefined and flashing languors, to unthinkable urgencies. . . . With a cry he leapt to her, clasped her, felt her young strength and lissome grace yield to his enfoldment. . . . Outside the great wind possessed the world, full of the turbulence, the fever, the unassuaged desire of Spring, the *allegro furioso* of the elements, and through it pierced the unbearable sweetness of the stringed melody."

Well, sir, that would seem to be it. By all the ordinary rules of physiology and pulp fiction, Pat and Cary should have been allowed at this juncture to retire tranquilly to the Fruit of the Loom without let or hindrance and frisk as they pleased. But Fabian, in inverse ratio to the reader, is just getting interested in his characters and figuring out new ways to frustrate them. They keep everlastingly melting into scorching embraces and springing apart the moment a rapprochement impends between them. She wants, he don't want; he wants, she don't want—your exasperation eventually reaches such a pitch that you would like to knock their heads together and lock them up in a motel with a copy of van der Velde's *Ideal Marriage*. The subplot bumbles in at intervals, adding to the general obfuscation a thwarted intrigue involving Dee Fentriss and a British electrician stylishly named Stanley Wollaston. At last, with the rueful conclusion: "We're terrible boobs, Cary. . . . Let's stop it"—a suggestion hardly calculated to provoke a quarrel with me—Pat sends her lover away to think things out and pins her affections on Leo Stenak, a brilliant violinist. This peters out when she discovers that he washes infrequently ("She forgot the genius, the inner fire; beheld only the outer shell, uncouth, pulpy, nauseous to her senses"), and she becomes affianced to Monty Standish, a Princeton football idol whose personal daintiness is beyond reproach. And then, in a smashing climax, so suspenseful that the least snore is liable to disrupt the delicate balance of his yarn, Fabian deftly turns the tables. Cary appears with the providential news that his wife has freed him, lips settle down to an uninterrupted feast, and, oblivious of the dead and dying syntax about them, the lovers go forth in search of Ben Lindsey and a companionate marriage.

It may be only a coincidence, but for a whole day after rereading *Flaming Youth*, my pupils were so dilated that you would have sworn I had been using belladonna. My complexion, though somewhat ruddier, recalled Bartholomew Sholto's in *The Sign of the Four* as he lay transfixed by an aboriginal dart that fateful night at Pondicherry Lodge. Luckily, I managed to work out a simple, effective treatment I can pass on to anyone afflicted with stardust poisoning. All you need is an eyedropper, enough kerosene to saturate an average three-hundred-and-thirty-six-page romance, and a match. A darkened room, for lying down in afterward, is nice but not absolutely essential. Just keep your eyes peeled, your nose clean, and avoid doctors and novels written by doctors. When you're over forty, one extra bumper of overripe beauty can do you in.

Lady, Play Your Endocrines

IN THE latter half of 1925, when the spirit of François Villon still hovered over the Jumble Shop and no poetry evening was complete without Eli Siegel declaiming "Hot Afternoons Have Been in Montana," I shared with another impecunious prospector and fellow-alumnus from Brown a cavernous, dingy room on West Eighth Street, in the Village. Four flights up and colder than the Kirghiz Steppe, it was nevertheless pervaded by a tropical effluvium from the dry cleaner's on the ground floor and commanded an unobstructed view of five restaurants neither of us could afford to patronize. We took our meals, to use a very loose designation, at a cruller shop down the block, and while we succeeded in sustaining life, I have ever since managed to view doughnuts with a measure of stoicism. Montague Adair, my roommate, was one of those unique personalities whose exteriors are as distinguished as their names. His classic features, seemingly chiseled of purest Parian marble, sable hair that put the raven's wing to shame, and an air of Beardsleyesque melancholy had already devastated innumerable coeds, and, to judge from the lipsticks and bobby pins strewn about when one returned from an enforced evening's stroll, he was by way of becoming the outstanding nympholept of the downtown metropolitan area.

A slim purse, however, pretty well circumscribed our social life, and our leisure was usually spent at home reading. Montague, employed on a garment-trade newspaper, dreamed of one day blossoming into a writer of pulp fiction. Consequently, he made a point of keeping abreast of *Argosy*, *Flynn's*, *Cupid's Diary*, *Railroad Stories*, and similar periodicals—solely to study their plot techniques, he was quick to assure you, for he professed to scorn their sleazy, infantile philosophy. Sprawled in a rump-sprung Morris chair, his forehead contorted in a scowl of concentration, Montague nightly applied himself to the incredible villainies and *galanteries* of the pulps. Some cut-rate leech having told him shortly before that he was anemic, my roommate was also valiantly attempting to restore his tissue tone. In the course of his evening's homework, he would work his way through a pint container of vanilla ice cream and a box of graham crackers, eating with a deliberate, maddening obduracy that in time began to take its toll of my nerves. I used to loll across the room from him on a Roman day bed covered in monk's cloth, struggling to fix my mind on the novel I was reading, but sooner or later I would detect myself staring at him in fascinated revulsion. He ate the ice cream with the small, flat wooden paddle supplied by the drugstore, sluggishly scooping up a gob, placing the paddle on his tongue, and allowing the cream to disintegrate, his slightly bovine eyes never straying from the printed page. This grisly ritual, varied only by an occasional tangerine, whose stringy rind he braided into a torque and left in the ashtray, eventually became a fixation with me. Each time he raised the paddle to his lips, I could almost taste its dry, grainy surface myself; beads of sweat the size of Malaga grapes stood forth on my brow and I ground my nails into my palms to keep from crying out. At last, the floodgates gave way. One night, I leaped to my feet, cut loose with a falsetto paraphrase of *Hedda Gabler*, and ran screaming down Macdougal Street. The next day, I moved into a single bedroom at the West Side Y.M.C.A.

I hardly expected that bittersweet epoch to return with such poignancy when, a few days ago, I picked Gertrude Atherton's *Black Oxen* out of a second-hand bin on Fourth Avenue. Then, as I thumbed through it, with the Cyclops eye of the bookseller behind the plate glass challenging me to steal it, I remembered it as the great novel of my *fin-de-siècle* period. For one freezing instant, I was propelled backward in time to my spavined day bed, torn between Mrs. Atherton's glandular *Spielerei* and Montague's odious paddle. Every dictate of good sense warned me that the prudent course would be to let the past bury its dead, flee to a Turkish bath, and go on a brannigan, but did I do it? Ah, no—I had to buy the book yet.

Black Oxen, published in 1923, achieved thirteen editions in nine months, disrupted bridge luncheons and dinner parties the country over, made its author one of the most talked-of women of the century, and brought to movie stardom a lady who, after twenty-five years, is still my dream boat. To those who remember Corinne Griffith as the Countess Marie Zattiany in the film version, I need say no more; if any gentlemen are minded to form a club like the Junta in *Zuleika Dobson*, dedicated to celebrating her sempiternal loveliness, I place at their disposal my rooms at the Albany. Rereading *Black Oxen* today, I find it difficult to be objective. I cannot altogether divorce the incomparable luster of

Miss Griffith's eyes, her porcelain fragility, from the heroine of the novel, and if I should occasionally whinny or *segue* into the opening bars of "Yearning," I trust it will be taken in good part.

Ponce de León's fountain has always found favor with the popular imagination, and in choosing its modern counterpart, gland rejuvenation, as her theme, Mrs. Atherton was a sly mongoose. Her tale begins at a fashionable first night, at which we are introduced to Lee Clavering, top-flight columnist and former dramatic critic. Clavering is a schoolgirl's dream, an alloy of Heathcliff, Conrad Veidt, and Jinx Falkenburg's brother. He is thirty-four, has a long, lounging body, a dark, saturnine face, and steel-blue eyes, and, to list but four of the labels used to tag him, is fastidious, cynical, morose, and mysterious. It is superfluous to add (though the author does, and at length) that he is a thoroughgoing misogynist. Well, Mac, you must be intuitive. As the first act draws to a close, he spies in front of him a head of hair "the color of warm ashes" and "no more than a glimpse of a white neck and a suggestion of sloping shoulders." "Rather rare those, nowadays," observes Clavering to himself—a sentiment I found baffling, for most heads I recall in the twenties were part of a set that included neck and shoulders. A few minutes later, during the intermission, their owner rises and coolly scrutinizes the audience through her opera glasses. Space precludes my tabulating the niceties of her face and figure, but I may assure the reader that she's a dilly. She wears a dress of white jet, long white gloves, and a triple string of pearls whose radiance is dimmed by her eyes: "They were very dark gray eyes, Greek in the curve of the lid, and inconceivably wise, cold, disillusioned." The problem is posed; the players attend. White captures Black in an unspecified number of moves, and damn'd be he that first cries, "Hold, enough."

Once started, the plot of *Black Oxen* picks up speed like a ruptured toboggan. In the theater lobby, Clavering runs into Charles Dinwiddie, an elderly clubman and a relative of his, who likewise has been struck all of a heap, but for quite another reason. "Thirty-odd years ago," he informs Clavering, "any one of us old chaps would have told you she was Mary Ogden, and like as not raised his hat. She was the beauty and belle of her day. But she married a Hungarian diplomat, Count Zattiany, when she was twenty-four, and deserted us." Before long, the lady begins exciting popular attention as well; society and the press boil with speculation and rumor about her identity. It is pertinent to note here what a flattering level of literacy Mrs. Atherton ascribes to the journalism of the Jazz Age: "The columnists had commented on her. One had indited ten lines of free verse in her honor, another had soared on the wings of seventeenth-century English into a panegyric on her beauty and her halo of mystery. A poet-editor-wit had cleped her 'The Silent Drama.'" The last verb, incidentally, is a fair sample of Mrs. Atherton's relish for the recherché, or uptown, word. She speaks elsewhere of a "rubescent Socialist," "rhinocerene hides," and a "debauched gerontic virgin."

Despite concerted efforts of Dinwiddie and Mrs. Oglethorpe, a dowager who grew up with Mary Ogden, to probe the mystery surrounding the fair stranger, she remains a fascinating enigma. She turns up at every first night, fanning Clavering's infatuation to white heat as the weeks pass. "She never rose in her seat again, and, indeed, seemed to seek inconspicuousness, but she was always in the second or third row of the orchestra, and she wore a different gown on each occasion." A rather ineffectual method of shunning the limelight, if I may say so; it would probably have caused less comment if she had worn a fringed lampshade on her head, and a pair of snowshoes. Finally, Clavering follows her one evening to her mansion on Murray Hill. To his elation, she is not unaware of his interest. "Oh, it is you," she says with a faint smile. "I forgot my key and I cannot make anyone hear the bell. The servants sleep on the top floor, and of course like logs." Her cavalier obligingly kicks in a windowpane, and she rewards him with sandwiches and whiskey in the library, where a log is burning on the hearth—presumably some servant incapable of reaching the top floor. Out of this session comes her declaration that she is yet another Countess Zattiany, a third cousin of Mary Ogden, who, she says, is in a Vienna sanitarium. Clavering is so enamored of her Old World charm, whatever her identity, that, on reaching the sidewalk, he stands guard over the house for two hours. The heroes of current fiction exhibit such constancy all too seldom. In a dozen hardboiled novels I could name, girls have lavished lots more than sandwiches and whiskey without any token of devotion beyond a glancing peck on the cheek.

As the story progresses and Clavering lays siege to the countess, it grows rapidly apparent that she is a *femme du monde* of vast experience for a person in her early thirties, one who has enjoyed social triumphs and knows them to be illusory. "Luncheons! Dinners! Balls! I was surfeited before the war," she observes scornfully on being pressed to re-enter society. When Clavering admiringly remarks that she must have distinguished herself abroad, she assents with fetching candor: "Oh, yes. Once an entire house—it was at the opera—rose as I entered my box at the end of the first act." Besides betraying an intimate knowledge of three decades of European diplomacy, Mme. Zattiany also drops several casual hints about Dr. Steinach, the noted Viennese endocrinologist, which should tip her mitt to the least observant, but her beau grimly refuses to tumble. For a columnist-critic represented as a blend of Jimmie Fidler and James Gibbons Huneker, Clavering is wondrously obtuse. He bumbles around with no suspicion that he has pinned his affections on a miracle of surgery, attributing her witchery to everything but the obvious medical reason. One evening, for example, they are dining at her home. "She was eating her oysters daintily and giving him the benefit of her dark brown eyelashes," states the narrative, breeding envy in those of us who have trouble gracefully manipulating our lashes, let alone our oysters. This inexplicably provokes from Clavering a genealogical litany establishing Mme. Zattiany as a Nordic princess. "Oh, yes, you are a case of atavism, no doubt," he assures her. "I can see you sweeping northward over the steppes of Russia as the ice-caps retreated . . . re-embodied on the Baltic coast or the shores of the North Sea . . . sleeping for ages in one of the Megaliths, to rise again a daughter of the Brythons, or of a Norse Viking . . . west into Anglia to appear once more as a Priestess of the Druids chaunting in a sacred grove . . . or as Boadicea—who knows!"

The upshot of these dithyrambs is, of course, a proposal of marriage, which ultimately compels the countess to publicly divulge her secret; namely, that she is the true Countess Zattiany (née Mary Ogden), that she is crowding fifty-eight, and that her pristine zip has been rekindled at Professor Steinach's gland parlors in Vienna. Clavering's ardor abates temporarily; he undergoes a phase of irresolution and soul-searching wherein his work suffers, but he gamely meets his obligations: "He avoided the office and wrote his column at home. Luckily a favorite old comedian had died recently. He could fill up with reminiscence and anecdote." Providential indeed, and a striking demonstration of the truth of a pair of old adages about silver linings and ill winds. At any rate, love vanquishes his misgivings, and, proposing again to the countess, who by now is a national sensation comparable to the flying saucers, he is accepted. Just as the blissful couple are making plans for a honeymoon at a shoe box in the Dolomites (it may have been a shooting box; frankly, I had no time for technicalities at this advanced stage of the story), the third leg of the triangle comes into view. Prince Moritz Franz Ernest Felix von Hohenhauer, an elder statesman of the Austrian Empire and former lover of the *Gräfin*, arrives in New York on business of state. He pursues his ex-sweetheart to a bohemian retreat in the Adirondacks, to which Clavering has spirited her, and, in the following majestic mouthful, tries to dissuade her from the marriage: "Your revivified glands have restored to you the appearance and the strength of youth, but although you have played with a role that appealed to your vanity, to your histrionic powers—with yourself as chief audience—your natural desire to see if you could not be—to yourself, again—as young as you appear, you have no more illusion in your soul than when you were a withered old woman in Vienna." Whether by his logic or by his tortured grammar, the Prince succeeds in casting a blight on the romance, and the book closes on a lovers' renunciation in Central Park as sweet as any *Linzer Torte* in Rumpelmayer's. Or, should I say, as any wooden paddleful of vanilla ice cream slowly dissolving on the tongue.

If my sentimental return to *Black Oxen* had any aftermath other than biliousness, it reminded me how negligent I have been of late toward my ductless glands. The last time I visited Los Angeles, there was a shop on South Figueroa in whose window was a mound of assorted jelly beans marked "Fancy male hormones and pep glands—$1.49 the pound." My next trip through, I figure to latch onto a little bag of those—say, ten cents' worth. So if you see a middle-aged chap with a dark, saturnine face, fastidious and morose, swinging around the shelves of your second-hand bookshop and chattering like a gibbon, you'll know who it is. But don't think you've got a Chinaman's chance, girls. His heart's still pledged to Corinne Griffith.

Great Aches from
Little Boudoirs Grow

WHENEVER I stretch out before my incinerator, churchwarden in hand, and, staring reflectively into the dying embers, take
inventory of my mottled past, I inevitably hark back to a period,
in the spring of 1926, that in many ways was the most romantic
of my life. I was, in that turbulent and frisky epoch, an artist of
sorts, specializing in neo-primitive woodcuts of a heavily waggish
nature that appeared with chilling infrequency in a moribund
comic magazine. It was a hard dollar, but it allowed me to stay in
bed until noon, and I was able to get by with half as many haircuts
as my conventional friends above Fourteenth Street. My atelier
was a second-floor rear bedroom in a handsome mansion on West
Ninth Street, temporarily let out to respectable bachelors during
the owner's absence abroad. In this sunny and reposeful chamber, I had set up my modest possessions: the draftsman's table
and tools of my trade; a rack of costly Dunhills I never smoked;
and a lamp made of a gigantic bottle, formerly an acid carboy, and
trimmed with an opaque parchment shade that effectively blan-
keted any light it gave. After pinning up a fast batik or two, I lent
further tone to the premises by shrouding the ceiling fixture with

one of those prickly, polyhedral glass lampshades esteemed in the Village, a lethal contraption that was forever gouging furrows in my scalp. It met its Waterloo the evening a young person from the *Garrick Gaieties*, in a corybantic mood, swung into a cancan and executed a kick worthy of La Goulue. The crash is said to have been audible in Romany Marie's, six blocks away.

I had not been installed in my diggings very long before I found that they were not ideally suited to provide the tranquillity I had hoped for. My windows overlooked a refuge for unwed mothers operated by the Florence Crittenton League, and almost every morning between four and six the wail of newborn infants reverberated from the chimney pots. Occasionally, of an afternoon, I beheld one of the ill-starred girls on the roof, scowling at me in what I interpreted as an accusatory manner, and although I had in no way contributed to her downfall, I was forced to draw the blinds before I could regain a measure of composure. Far more disturbing, however, was the behavior of the clientele attracted by the tenant of the studio above mine, a fashionable Austrian portrait painter. This worthy, a fraudulent dauber who had parlayed an aptitude for copying Boldini and Philip de László into an income of six figures, was the current *Wunderkind* of Park Avenue; the socially prominent streamed to his dais like pilgrims to the Kaaba in Mecca. The curb in front of the house was always choked with sleek, custom-built Panhards and Fiats, and hordes of ravishing ladies, enveloped in sables and redolent of patchouli, ceaselessly surged past my door. What with the squeals and giggles that floated down from the upper landing, the smack of garters playfully snapped, and pretty objurgations stifled by kisses, I was in such a constant state of cacoëthes that I shrank to welterweight in a fortnight.

It would be unfair, though, to hold the painter entirely culpable for my condition; a good share of it was caused by a novel I was bewitched with at the time—Maxwell Bodenheim's *Replenishing Jessica*. Its publication, it will be recalled, aroused a major scandal hardly surpassed by *Lady Chatterley's Lover*. Determined efforts were made to suppress it, and it eventually gave rise to Jimmy Walker's celebrated dictum that no girl has ever been seduced by a book. Whether the *mot* was confirmed by medical testimony, I cannot remember, but in one immature reader, at least, *Replenishing Jessica* created all the symptoms of breakbone fever. So much so, in fact, that prior to a nostalgic reunion with it several days ago, I fortified myself with a half grain of codeine. I need not have bothered. Time, the great analgesic, had forestalled me.

To call the pattern of Mr. Bodenheim's story simple would be like referring to St. Peter's as roomy or Lake Huron as moist; "elementary" sums it up rather more succinctly. Condensed to its essence, *Replenishing Jessica* is an odyssey of the bedtime hazards of a young lady of fashion bent on exploring her potentialities. Jessica Maringold is the twenty-three-year-old daughter of a real-estate millionaire, willful, perverse, alternately racked by an impulse to bundle and a hankering for the arts. Without any tedious preliminaries, she weighs in on the very first page perched on a piano bench near a stockbroker named Theodore Purrel, for whom she is playing "one of Satie's light affairs." "She was a little above medium height, with a body that was quite plump between the hips and upper thighs," the author recounts, exhibiting a gusto for anatomical detail that often threatens to swamp his narrative. Purrel receives a similarly severe appraisal: "He was a tall man, just above thirty years, and he had the body of an athlete beginning to deteriorate—the first sign of a paunch and too much fat on his legs." With all this lard in proximity, it is preordained that high jinks will ensue, and they do—cataclysmically. "His fingers enveloped the fullness of her breasts quite as a boy grasps soap-bubbles and marvels at their intact resistance." The soap bubbles I grasped as a boy were not distinguished for their elasticity, but they may have been more resilient in Mr. Bodenheim's youth. Meanwhile, during these gymnastics Jessica surrenders herself to typically girlish musings. "She remembered the one night in which she had given herself to him. . . . She knew that Purrel would grasp her, and she reflected on some way of merrily repulsing him, such as pulling his tie, wrenching his nose, tickling his ears." Unluckily, the delaying action had been futile, and Purrel managed to exact his tribute. Now, however, he impresses her as a dull, self-confident libertine, an estimate borne out by his Philistine rejection of her intellect. "I wish you'd give this mind stuff a rest. . . . It doesn't take much brains to smear a little paint on canvas and knock around with a bunch of long-haired mutts. . . . I may not be a world-beater but I've run up a fat bank account in the last eight years and you can't do *that* on an empty head." The struggle between Theodore's animal appeal and Jessica's spiritual nature is resolved fortuitously. "The frame of the piano, below the keys, was pressing into her lower spine, like an absurd remonstrance that made her mood prosaic in the passing of a second," Bodenheim explains, adding with magisterial portentousness, "The greatest love can be turned in a thrice [*sic*] to the silliest of frauds by a breaking chair, or the prolonged creaking of a couch." When the lust has blown away, Jessica is safe in her bedroom and her admirer presumably on his way to a cold shower. "Purrel felt feverish and thwarted without knowing why," says the text, though any reasonably alert chimpanzee of three could have furnished him a working hypothesis.

Jessica's next sexual skirmish takes place at twilight the following afternoon, in the studio of Kurt Salburg, a dour Alsatian painter who addresses her as "*Liebchen*" and subjects her virtue, or what's left of it, to a coarse, Teutonic onslaught. His brutal importunities, unaccompanied by the slightest appeal to her soul, provoke her into withholding her favors, but she confers them a scant twenty-four hours later on Sydney Levine, a masterful criminal lawyer, who requisitions them in the terse, direct fashion of an Army quartermaster ordering sixty bags of mule feed. "I have wanted you for six months," Levine tells her. "I have no lies or romantic pretenses to give you. My love for you is entirely physical, and nothing except complete possession will satisfy it. . . . From now on, it would be impossible to control myself in your presence, and it will have to be everything or nothing." Their romp leaves Jessica remorseful and more frustrated than ever. Eschewing the opposite sex for three weeks, she stays glued to her easel, creating futuristic pictures apropos of which the author observes, "She had a moderate talent for painting." The sample he describes would appear to permit some room for discussion: ". . . two lavender pineapples, placed on each side of a slender, black and white vase, all of the articles standing on a dark red table that seemed about to fall on the cerise floor." Of course, there is always the possibility that Mr. Bodenheim is being sardonic, just as there is always the possibility that the Princess Igor Troubetzkoy is planning to leave me her stock in the five-and-ten-cent stores.

Ostensibly purified by her joust with the Muse, Jessica now retreads her steps to Salburg's studio to bedevil him a bit further. This time the lecherous Alsatian uses a more devious gambit to achieve his ends. He employs the infantile, or blubber-mouth, approach. "'If you should refuse me now, I would never live again,' he said, in a low voice. 'Never, never . . . I am helpless and frightened, Jessica.' His words had a defenceless quiver that could not be disbelieved. . . . A disrobed and frantic boy was speaking his fear that she might whip his naked breast." Following a rough-and-tumble interlude, the participants spend the evening at a *Nachtlokal* with Purrel, whom Jessica pits against Salburg to keep things humming. In the resulting scrimmage, the stockbroker draws first claret; Jessica is repelled by the artist's craven behavior and, dismissing her flames as bullies and cowards, decides to pop over to Europe and see what beaux are available in England. There is a vignette of her, aboard ship, calculated to awake tender memories in the older girls: "She was dressed in dark purple organdy with white rosettes at the waist, stockings and shoes of the same purple hue, a long, thin cape of white velvet, and a pale straw turban trimmed with black satin." It is a coincidence worth recording that the young person from the *Garrick Gaieties* referred to earlier wore exactly this costume when she danced the cancan in my web. Naturally, she removed the long, thin cape of white velvet to facilitate her kick at the lamp, but in every other respect her ensemble was identical. Sort of spooky, when you come to think of it.

Having installed herself in an apartment in Chelsea, Jessica plunges intrepidly into the bohemian whirl of London, keeping a weather eye out for brainy males. At the 1919 Club, a rendez-vous so named "in commemoration of a Russian revolution"—an aside that pricks your curiosity as to which one the author means—she encounters four. They are (disguised under impenetrable pseudonyms) Ramsay MacDonald, the Sitwell brothers, and Aldous Huxley, but, regrettable to say, no pyrotechnics of note occur. At last, the situation brightens. One evening, Jessica finds herself in her flat discussing Havelock Ellis with a personable ex-officer named Robert Chamberlain, ". . . and during the course of the talk Jessica partly unloosened her heliotrope blouse because of the warmness of the room, and sprawled at ease on a couch without a thought of sensual invitation." Innocent as the gesture is, Chamberlain in his crass, masculine way misconstrues it. "His confidently thoughtful mood was shattered, and for the first time he looked steadily at the tapering, disciplined curve of her legs, slowly losing their plumpness as their lines fell to her ankles, and half revealed by her raised, white skirt; and the sloping narrowness of her shoulders, and her small-lipped, impishly not quite round face that was glinting and tenuous in the moderated light of the room." But the foregoing is merely a feint on Bodenheim's part, and two months of interminable palaver are necessary before his creatures coalesce to make great music. The slow buildup plainly does much to intensify Chamberlain's fervor: "His mind changed to a fire that burned without glowing—a black heat—and his emotions were dervishes." Once the pair wind up in the percale division, the same old sense of disillusion begins gnawing at Jessica. A week of stormy bliss and she is off to New York again, hastily sandwiching in a last-minute affair with Joseph Israel, a London real-estate broker.

The concluding fifty pages of *Replenishing Jessica* cover a span of approximately six years and vibrate with the tension of high-speed oatmeal. Jessica passes through a succession of lovers (including poets, musical-comedy stars, and other migratory workers), marries and discards Purrel, and inherits four million dollars, zestfully described as composed of real estate, bonds, and cash. (Offhand, I cannot recall another novel in which the scarlet threads of sex and real estate are so inextricably interwoven. It's like a union of Fanny Hill and Bing & Bing.) All these stimulating experiences, nevertheless, are no more than "a few snatchings at stars that turned out to be cloth ones sewed to the blue top of a circus tent," though one suspects a handful of the spangles may have been negotiable. Tired of drifting about the capitals of Europe and unable to find a mate who offers the ideal blend of sensuality and savvy, she devotes herself to teaching children to paint at an East Side settlement house. Here, among the lavender pineapples she is midwifing, she meets a saintly, partially deformed type given to reading Flaubert and writing aesthetic critiques. His luxuriant brown beard, exalted eyes, and general Dostoevskian halo augur well, and as the flyleaves loom, Jessica's saga ends with an elegiac quaver reminiscent of a Jesse Crawford organ solo.

Every book of consequence ultimately produces lesser works that bear its influence, and *Replenishing Jessica* is no exception. As collateral reading, I can recommend a small semi-scientific monograph I myself recently helped to prepare. It concerns itself with the peculiar interaction of codeine and ennui on a white hysteroid male of forty-four exposed to a bookful of erotic fancies. Unlike the average hypnotic subject, the central character was fully conscious at all times, even while asleep. He ate a banana, flung the skin out of the window, flung the book after the skin, and was with difficulty restrained from following. It sounds technical but it really isn't. It's an absorbing document, and above all it's as clean as a whistle. Not a single bit of smooching in it from start to finish. I made certain of *that*.

Antic Hey-Hey

PERHAPS the saltiest observation Max Beerbohm made in *Seven Men*, a book whose saline content has remained as high and delightful as it was on its appearance thirty years ago, occurs in that matchless story of a literary vendetta, "Hilary Maltby and Stephen Braxton." Writing about the preoccupation of contemporary novelists with sprites and woodland gods—Maltby, it will be recalled, was the author of *Ariel in Mayfair* and Braxton of *A Faun in the Cotswolds*—Beerbohm remarked, "From the time of Nathaniel Hawthorne to the outbreak of the war, current literature did not suffer from any lack of fauns." I suppose this reflection has always struck me as especially astute because when I originally encountered it, back in 1923, I happened to be in a milieu where satyrs and dryads, Silenus and Bacchic revels, were as common as cattails in a Jersey swamp. Its impact was heightened, moreover, by the fact that I was just convalescing (although for a while my reason was despaired of) from the effects of a tumultuous, beauty-bound best seller of the period called *Wife of the Centaur*, by Cyril Hume.

The place was Brown University, and the particular focus of all this mythological activity was a literary magazine by the name of *Casements*, on whose staff I had a brief, precarious toehold as assistant art editor. At least three-quarters of the text of *Casements* each month was made up of villanelles, rondels, pantoums, and ballades in which Pan pursued laughing nymphs through leafy bowers, and it was my job to provide decorative headings and tail-pieces to complement them. Fortunately, I had a steady hand and an adequate supply of tracing paper, and if my superiors had not accidentally stumbled on the two albums of Aubrey Beardsley I was cribbing my drawings from, I might have earned an enviable reputation.

My short and brilliant tenure had one positive result, how-ever; I finally discovered what was inspiring the Arcadian jingles I illustrated. One afternoon, while dawdling around the dormi-tory room of our chief troubadour and waiting for him to shellac a madrigal about cloven hoofs in the boscage, I picked up a novel bound in orange and gold and read a passage he had underscored. "Ho!" it ran. "The centaur is born! Child's body and colt's body, birth-wet and asprawl in the ferns. What mother will nourish this wild thing? Who will foster this beast-god? Where will he grow? In what strange cavern will he make his bed, dreaming his amazing dreams? What shaggy tutor will teach him as he lolls with his head on nature's breast? What mortal maid will he carry away to his upland pastures in terror and delight?"

"Hot puppies!" I burst out excitedly. "This isn't prose—it's fro-zen music! The gink who wrote this is the bee's knees!"

"Yes, yes," said the poet guiltily, plucking the book out of my hands. "I—er—I haven't read it myself, but I guess it's had a wide influence." It was a Freudian slip on his part, which some instinct told me was worth investigating, and when I did, my sus-picions were confirmed. Not only he but practically every bard on *Casements* had been using *Wife of the Centaur* as a water hole. The opportunities for blackmail were, of course, illimitable, and had my own nose been clean (the Beardsley complication was just breaking), I might have taken advantage of them. The truth is, though, that on reading the book I succumbed to its witchery so completely that I, too, began writing villanelles and pantoums in the same idiom. Sad to say, they never saw printer's ink; my colleagues, jealous of the applause the verses might excite, stopped publishing *Casements* altogether, and overnight a potential Wordsworth again became a drab little sophomore.

A week or so ago, standing with nostrils atwitch and a pocketful of rusty change over the bargain table of a Fifty-ninth Street bookstore, I spotted a copy of Mr. Hume's chef-d'oeuvre and, unable to resist a cut-rate sentimental pilgrimage into the past, gave it a home. Its effect, after a lapse of twenty-seven years, was not quite as dynamic as I had anticipated. Rather than quickening me to an orgy of spondees and dactyls, it slowed down my heartbeat to that of a turtle's and enveloped me in a profound slumber under a grape arbor, where I narrowly escaped being consumed by a colony of ants. It may sound unfair to suggest that they were attracted by the rich and sticky imagery of the book, but from now on I plan to restrict my open-air reading to the *World Almanac*, with a Flit gun cocked across my knee to repel browsers.

Since *Wife of the Centaur* is the tale of a sensitive boy who grows up to be a poet, it quite properly begins with a salvo of rapturous and yeasty verse to help you adjust your emotional sights. The following, one of several quatrains introducing a fifty-page pastiche of Jeffrey Dwyer's childhood, gives a hasty but reliable preview of the feature picture:

> *The centaurs awoke! they aroused from their beds of pine,*
> *Their long flanks hoary with dew, and their eyes deep-drowned*
> *In the primal slumber of stones, stirred bright to the shine!*
> *And they stamped with their hooves, and their gallop abased*
>   *the ground!*

Jeffrey, it is shortly established, is an infant centaur, in what might be described as cushy circumstances; he attends an exclusive private school in Connecticut, preparing for Yale, and, when not saturating himself in *The Oxford Book of English Verse*, struggles tormentedly under the lash of awakening sex. The description of the process discloses him to be a pretty full-blooded lad: "Lean desire wrapped his body in taut coils, oppressing him like pain. . . . Lust was a blind force, immeasurable, overwhelming, irresistible as a toppling wall of black water. . . . And desire, the gaunt beast, buffeted and shook him. . . . 'God! God!' . . . The air was a voice that hissed hot promises of forbidden mysteries, the trees were erotic minstrels singing old songs of shameful loves." Luckily for Jeffrey, if not for the reader, his adolescent libido is channeled into writing verse before it lays waste the Nutmeg State, and while the samples furnished are hardly calculated to set the Housatonic on fire—packed as they are with fantasies of whitely radiant madonnas with golden coils of hair and cherry-red lips moving in strange benedictions—it is clear that Calliope has destined the youngster for the business end of a quill.

The heroine of the book, a conventional maiden named Joan Converse, in the same affluent social stratum, now makes her advent with a clash of cymbals and another fifty pages of adolescent background. Joan's sexual yearnings do not seem quite as turbulent as Jeffrey's, but she gets a symbolical sendoff just as rousing: "Ohé hamadryad, lurking in yon covert of ruddy sumac, are your cheeks red with remembered dreaming? Hark! Hark, little maid with the limbs of a slim cascade—hark, for the young centaur tramples and neighs along the wooded hillside, no longer far away. And you do not flee, little maid with your rose-petal cheeks? Ah, the centaur! Ho, hamadryad!" It is futile to begin slavering and speculating on the explosion the two will eventually create, though, because their paths do not converge for years, and by the time they do, at a Long Island house party, the third leg of the triangle is already in place. Jeffrey, during the interval, has been distinguishing himself at Yale as a poet and tosspot, and is currently dangling after Inez Martin, a heartless flirt whose eyes range from clear gray to transparent green with her varying moods. "She's a willow beside a brook of running water, and the sun on both," the poet epitomizes her to Joan, brokenly recounting the indignities Inez has subjected him to. Irksome as the maternal role is, Joan sensibly bides her time and is rewarded in the Easter vacation, when Jeffrey buckles under her own glamour in the rear seat of a Stutz. He kisses her roughly, impetuously; as she goes faint at the contact of his slim, strong hands, she notices that "they seemed to have an eager, fine life of their own. Tense and flexible and swift as blood horses." Much to Joan's chagrin, alas, it is merely a routine workout for the ponies. Reining them in before they can bolt, Jeffrey warns her that something horrible might have happened, that she must never let anyone again kiss her in such abandoned fashion. "'Me least of all,' he said harshly. Then he bent down and kissed the cool palm of her hand." And so, in a bittersweet dying fall that combines echoes of Havre de Grace, Jergens Lotion, and the code of a Yale gentleman, is born the romance of Joan Converse, occupation hamadryad, and Jeffrey Dwyer, jongleur and centaur.

Actually, despite all the preliminary huffing and puffing, nothing concrete develops between them in the ensuing third of the story, for Jeffrey still has to fight the First World War and purge Inez from his system. He cleans up the first, and obviously easier, assignment in a brisk ten pages, throws himself into a journalistic career, and makes a superhuman but fruitless pitch for Joan's rival. How greatly she disturbs him may be gauged from this saucy vignette: "Her blouse was deeply opened at the neck, showing a long V of glowing flesh with a faint shadow at the point. One foot was drawn up under her and Jeffrey caught a glimpse of a rosy knee with the stocking rolled below it. . . . Happiness pierced him suddenly like a flaming sword. His pulses beat to the rhythm of a wild prothalamion. . . . He! For him! He was to explore the shrouded mysteries that dwelt behind her eyes. Her Venus body and the youth of it, the promises he read in the sultry curves of her mouth . . . these were his to take and hold like a cup, to drink deep. . . ." The goodies, maddeningly, remain just out of reach; Inez has pledged herself to a wastrel named Jack Todd, and, sick with disillusion, Jeffrey plunges into a stormy cycle of wenching and boozing that climaxes in the arms of a lady of the town. Slowly and painfully, his equilibrium returns, a salvage operation that calls forth fresh flights of lyricism: "Now is the centaur weary of men and men's ways. . . . Centaur, is your beast's spirit broken? Is your man's heart crushed utterly? No! For now the centaur shouts anew his loud defiance! . . . I will go back again to taste the bright hill-water of my colthood and my nostrils shall know as of old the thin air of my mountain realms. I shall lie upon a bed of ferns under familiar constellations. . . . In the still of the night, in an hour when quiet comes upon the crickets and all the little creatures of the dark, I shall reach up with my hand and pluck that round honeycomb, the moon, out of the sky to feed my hunger."

Reduced to prosaic, taxpayer's lingo, this means that Jeffrey goes back to his prep school, engages in a purifying bull session with the headmaster, sobers up, finishes a novel called "Squads Right About" debunking war, and publishes it to wide critical acclaim. Joan, who meanwhile has lain obligingly dormant for a hundred pages waiting for her swain to unsnarl his glands, hereupon pops back into view. Just why she and Jeffrey should plight their troth at the Museum of Natural History, I was unable to fathom, except that it affords the hero an opportunity to indulge in some verbal pyrotechnics on science—or, rather, his conception of it. "Geology, Joan!" he exclaims. "God, but I love geology! Astronomy! The gorgeous tremendousness of it! Science for gods! . . . Your mind goes tramping through space like a hobo in spring, with spiral nebulas trailing at its ankles like gobs of cobwebs. You want to howl and kick suns around because then you realize that the human mind is the greatest created thing." At any rate, after a plethora of similar brainy generalizations, Jeffrey providentially runs out of saliva, and the two dissolve into an embrace that leads to the altar and the next movement of the symphony, a section stylishly entitled "Lilith's Garden."

"Lilith's Garden" is ecstasy unconfined by whalebone, chaperone, or censor, a honeymoon that makes most other fictional ones I can recall seem vapid by comparison. The newlyweds spend it at a seaside cottage on Long Island, whooping around the dunes and behaving in a thoroughly heathen and unfettered fashion: "At night on the beach, he would suddenly make a horrible face and howl, 'I'm a remora!' or 'I'm a mandrake!' or even 'I'm a Calvin-ist!' Then he would growl and come after her in great fantastic leaps, flinging out his arms and legs and she would squeal and try to double back to the deserted steamer rug." The proximity of salt water, naturally, brings on a whole new rush of metaphor, and the hamadryad switches into a mermaid: "And when he kissed her mouth he tasted the brine of the deep places where her home was; and her dipping arms crept around his neck to draw him under and carry him down forever to a palace of pale coral where fish darted like birds in a garden." As if these quincelike frivolities were already not sufficient to pucker up one's lips, they are punc-tuated by scolding comments from an old Irish retainer of Joan's playfully known as Madsy, a dialectician of the school of Harrigan and Hart: "Didn't I hear the both of yez on the beach last night carryin' on like wild pagan creatures? Half the night you was up behavin' scandleous and undaicent as though there wasn't that much of a Christian soul between yez! . . . When you might better have been in your bed you was out on the sand there schreechin' like a pair of unredeemed catamounts. . . . Then *you*, Mr. Dwyer, takes and carries her upstairs, with the pair of yez drippin' like Tim Connel's ghost and him just after drownin' himself for havin' hit Father Mulligan a skelp wid an axe." Alanna, and 'tis with a sigh of relief and the divil's own skippin' of pages that you finally claw your way out of the tunnel of love.

The culmination of *Wife of the Centaur* may be one of the mildest in letters, but I was never so glad to see a culmination in my life. It is, of course, Inez, the girl with the chameleon eyes, who motivates it; Jeffrey has barely settled down on a Connecti-cut hilltop with his bride when the enchantress slinks back into the plot and everything goes haywire again. Night after night, the harassed poet patrols the countryside, waging a losing fight against her allure and addressing rhetorical questions to the heavens: "Must all true metal be tempered in flame? Is every birth a long agony? *Designer infinite. . . . Ah! must Thou char the wood ere Thou canst limn with it?*" Then, at very long last, comes blessed deliverance for all hands. Amid melting snows and adjectives, Jeffrey finds that the dross has burned away, and in a single burst of renewed creativeness composes two hundred and sixty lines of a saga called "The Brook." "God, Joan! I've never written anything like it in my life before! It's poetry . . . it's great poetry!" But whether it is or not will forever rest a secret, because at this juncture the reader is swept up on a mountainous comber boiling with allusions to Botticelli, Pallas Athene, and the old surefire thunder of centaur hoofs, and is washed up, weak as a kitten, in the end papers.

The reaction of a forty-five-year-old stomach to twenty-five-year-old brandy is a physiological certainty, but surprisingly little information exists on how that organ responds to novels of the same vintage. My subsequent history, therefore, may have a trifling clinical value. For thirty-six hours after completing *Wife of the Centaur*, I experienced intermittent queasiness, a tendency to howl "I'm a Philistine!" and an exaggerated revulsion for the printed page. A day or two later, while emptying a wheelbarrow of old books into a gully near my home, I saw (or thought I saw) a stout, bearded individual with four feet chasing a scantily clad maenad along a ridge. I returned home on the double and, having notified the local game warden, busied myself with indoor matters. Ever since, I have been hearing reedy sounds from the ridge, as of someone playing a rustic set of pipes. More than likely, the game warden got himself mixed up in a three-handed saturnalia and they're looking for a fourth. One of these evenings, as soon as I can get myself shod, I really must gallop up there and see.

Why, Doctor,
What Big Green Eyes You Have!

HALFWAY through the summer of 1916, I was living on the rim of Narragansett Bay, a fur-bearing adolescent with cheeks as yet unscarred by my first Durham Duplex razor, when I read a book that exerted a considerable influence on my bedtime habits. Up to then, I had slept in normal twelve-year-old fashion, with the lights full on, a blanket muffling my head from succubi and afreets, a chair wedged under the doorknob, and a complex network of strings stretched across the room in a way scientifically designed to entrap any trespasser, corporeal or not. On finishing the romance in question, however, I realized that the protection I had been relying on was woefully inadequate and that I had merely been crowding my luck. Every night thereafter, before retiring, I spent an extra half hour barricading the door with a chest of drawers, sprinkling tacks along the window sills, and strewing crumpled newspapers about the floor to warn me of approaching footsteps. As a minor added precaution, I slept under the bed, a ruse that did not make for refreshing slumber but at least threw my enemies off the scent. Whether it was constant vigilance or natural stamina, I somehow survived, and, indeed, received a surprising number of compliments on my appearance when I returned to grammar school that fall. I guess nobody in those parts had ever seen a boy with snow-white hair and a green skin.

Perhaps the hobgoblins who plagued me in that Rhode Island beach cottage were no more virulent than the reader's own childhood favorites, but the particular one I was introduced to in the book I've mentioned could hold up his head in any concourse of fiends. Even after thirty-five years, the lines that ushered him onstage still cause an involuntary shudder:

"Imagine a person, tall, lean and feline, high-shouldered, with a brow like Shakespeare and a face like Satan, a close-shaven skull, and long, magnetic eyes of the true cat-green. Invest him with all the cruel cunning of an entire Eastern race, accumulated in one giant intellect, with all the resources of science, past and present, with all the resources, if you will, of a wealthy government—which, however, already has denied all knowledge of his existence. . . . This man, whether a fanatic or a duly appointed agent, is, unquestionably, the most malign and formidable personality existing in the world today. He is a linguist who speaks with almost equal facility in any of the civilized languages, and in most of the barbaric. He is an adept in all the arts and sciences which a great university could teach him. He also is an adept in certain obscure arts and sciences which *no* university of today can teach. He has the brains of any three men of genius. . . . Imagine that awful being, and you have a mental picture of Dr. Fu-Manchu, the yellow peril incarnate in one man."

Yes, it is the reptilian Doctor himself, one of the most sinister figures ever to slither out of a novelist's cranium, and many a present-day comic book, if the truth were told, is indebted to his machinations, his underground laboratories, carnivorous orchids, rare Oriental poisons, dacoits, and stranglers. An authentic vampire in the great tradition, Fu-Manchu horrified the popular imagination in a long series of best sellers by Sax Rohmer, passed through several profitable reincarnations in Hollywood, and (I thought) retired to the limbo of the second-hand bookshop, remembered only by a few slippered pantaloons like me. Some while ago, though, a casual reference by my daughter to Thuggee over her morning oatmeal made me prick up my ears. On close questioning, I found she had been bedeviling herself with *The Mystery of Dr. Fu-Manchu*, the very volume that had induced my youthful fantods. I delivered a hypocritical little lecture, worthy of Pecksniff, in which I pointed out that Laurence Hope's *Indian Love* was far more suitable for her age level, and, confiscating the book, holed up for a retrospective look at it. I see now how phlegmatic I have become with advancing age. Apart from causing me to cry out occasionally in my sleep and populating my pillow with a swarm of nonexistent spiders, Rohmer's thriller was as abrasive to the nerves as a cup of Ovaltine.

The plot of *The Mystery of Dr. Fu-Manchu* is at once engagingly simple and monstrously confused. In essence, it is a duel of wits between the malevolent Celestial, who dreams of a world dominated by his countrymen, and Commissioner Nayland Smith, a purportedly brilliant sleuth, whose confidant, Dr. Petrie, serves as narrator. Fu-Manchu comes to England bent on the extermination of half a dozen distinguished Foreign Office servants, Orientalists, and other buttinskies privy to his scheme; Smith and Petrie constantly scud about in a webfooted attempt to warn the prey, who are usually defunct by the time they arrive, or busy themselves with being waylaid, sandbagged, drugged, kidnaped, poisoned, or garroted by Fu-Manchu's deputies. These assaults, however, are never downright lethal, for regularly, at the eleventh hour, a beautiful slave of Fu-Manchu named Kâramanèh betrays her master and delivers the pair from jeopardy. The story, consequently, has somewhat the same porous texture as a Pearl White serial. An episode may end with Smith and Petrie plummeting through a trap door to nameless horrors below; the next opens on them comfortably sipping whisky-and-soda in their chambers, analyzing their hairbreadth escape and speculating about the adversary's next move. To synopsize this kind of ectoplasmic yarn with any degree of fidelity would be to connive at criminal boredom, and I have no intention of doing so, but it might be fruitful to dip a spoon into the curry at random to gain some notion of its flavor.

Lest doubt prevail at the outset as to the utter malignancy of Fu-Manchu, the author catapults Nayland Smith into Petrie's rooms in the dead of night with the following portentous declaration of his purpose: "Petrie, I have traveled from Burma not in the interests of the British government merely, but in the interest of the entire white race, and I honestly believe—though I pray I may be wrong—that its survival depends largely on the success of my mission." Can Petrie, demands Smith, spare a few days from his medical duties for "the strangest business, I promise you, that ever was recorded in fact or fiction"? He gets the expected answer: "I agreed readily enough, for, unfortunately, my professional duties were not onerous." The alacrity with which doctors of that epoch deserted their practice has never ceased to impress me. Holmes had only to crook his finger and Watson went bowling away in a four-wheeler, leaving his patients to fend for themselves. If the foregoing is at all indicative, the mortality rate of London in the nineteen hundreds must have been appalling; the average physician seems to have spent much less time in diagnosis than in tiptoeing around Wapping Old Stairs with a dark lantern. The white race, apparently, was a lot tougher than one would suspect.

At any rate, the duo hasten forthwith to caution a worthy named Sir Crichton Davey that his life is in peril, and, predictably, discover him already cheesed off. His death, it develops, stemmed from a giant red centipede, lowered down the chimney of his study by Fu-Manchu's dacoits, regarding whom Smith makes the charmingly offhand statement "Oh, dacoity, though quiescent, is by no means extinct." Smith also seizes the opportunity to expatiate on the archcriminal in some delicious double-talk: "As to his mission among men. Why did M. Jules Furneaux fall dead in a Paris opera house? Because of heart failure? No! Because his last speech had shown that he held the key to the secret of Tongking. What became of the Grand Duke Stanislaus? Elopement? Suicide? Nothing of the kind. He alone was fully alive to Russia's growing peril. He alone knew the truth about Mongolia. Why was Sir Crichton Davey murdered? Because, had the work he was engaged upon ever seen the light, it would have shown him to be the only living Englishman who understood the importance of the Tibetan frontiers." In between these rhetorical flourishes, Petrie is accosted by Kâramanèh, Fu-Manchu's houri, who is bearing a deadly perfumed letter intended to destroy Smith. The device fails, but the encounter begets a romantic interest that saves Petrie's neck on his next excursion. Disguised as rough seafaring men, he and Smith have tracked down Fu-Manchu at Singapore Charlie's, an opium shop on the Thames dockside. Here, for the first time, Petrie gets a good hinge at the monster's eyes: ". . . their unique horror lay in a certain filminess (it made me think of the *membrana nictitans* in a bird) which, obscuring them as I threw wide the door, seemed to lift as I actually passed the threshold, revealing the eyes in all their brilliant viridescence." Before he can polish his ornithological metaphor, however, Petrie is plunged through a trap door into the river, the den goes up in flames, and it looks like curtains for the adventurous physician. But Providence, in the form of a hideous old Chinese, intervenes. Stripping off his ugly, grinning mask, he discloses himself as Kâramanèh; she extends her false pigtail to Petrie and, after pulling him to safety, melts into the night. It is at approximately this juncture that one begins to appreciate how lightly the laws of probability weighed on Sax Rohmer. Once you step with him into Never-Never Land, the grave's the limit, and no character is deemed extinct until you can use his skull as a paperweight.

Impatient at the snail's pace with which his conspiracy is maturing, Fu-Manchu now takes the buttons off the foils. He tries to abduct a missionary who has flummoxed his plans in China, but succeeds only in slaying the latter's collie and destroying his manservant's memory—on the whole, a pretty footling morning's work. He then pumps chlorine gas into a sarcophagus belonging to Sir Lionel Barton, a bothersome explorer, with correspondingly disappointing results; this time the bag is another collie—sorry, a coolie—and a no-account ginzo secretary.

The villain's next foray is more heartening. He manages to over-power Smith and Petrie by some unspecified means (undoubtedly the "rather rare essential oil" that Smith says he has met with before, "though never in Europe") and chains them up in his noisome cellars. The scene wherein he twits his captives has a nice poetic lilt: "A marmoset landed on the shoulder of Dr. Fu-Manchu and peered grotesquely into the dreadful yellow face. The Doctor raised his bony hand and fondled the little creature, crooning to it. 'One of my pets, Mr. Smith,' he said, suddenly opening his eyes fully so that they blazed like green lamps. 'I have others, equally useful. My scorpions—have you met my scorpions? No? My pythons and hamadryads? Then there are my fungi and my tiny allies, the bacilli. I have a collection in my laboratory quite unique. Have you ever visited Molokai, the leper island, Doctor? No? But Mr. Nayland Smith will be familiar with the asylum at Rangoon! And we must not forget my black spiders, with their diamond eyes—my spiders, that sit in the dark and watch—then leap!'" Yet, having labored to create so auspicious a buildup, the author inexplicably cheats his suspense and lets it go for naught. No sooner has Fu-Manchu turned his back to attend to a poisoned soufflé in the oven than Kâramanèh pops up and strikes off the prisoners' gyves, and the whole grisly quadrille starts all over again. Smith and Petrie, without so much as a change of deerstalker hats, nip away to warn another prospective victim, and run full tilt into a covey of *phansigars*, the religious stranglers familiar to devotees of the *American Weekly* as Thugs. They outwit them, to be sure, but the pace is beginning to tell on Petrie, who observes ruefully, "In retrospect, that restless time offers a chaotic prospect, with few peaceful spots amid its turmoils." Frankly, I don't know what Petrie is beefing about. My compassion goes out, rather, to his patients, whom I envision by now as driven by default to extracting their own tonsils and quarrying each other's gallstones. *They're* the ones who need sympathy, Petrie, old boy.

With puff adders, tarantulas, and highbinders blooming in every hedgerow, the hole-and-corner pursuit of Fu-Manchu drums along through the next hundred pages at about the same tempo, resolutely shying away from climaxes like Hindus from meat. Even the episode in which Smith and Petrie, through the good offices of Kâramanèh, eventually hold the Doctor at gun point aboard his floating laboratory in the Thames proves just a pretext for further bombination about those filmy greenish eyes; a shower of adjectives explodes in the reader's face, and he is whisked off on a hunt for certain stolen plans of an aero-torpedo, an interlude that veers dangerously close to the exploits of the indomitable Tom Swift. The sequence that follows, as rich in voodoo as it is innocent of logic, is heavily fraught with hypnosis, Fu-Manchu having unaccountably imprisoned a peer named Lord Southery and Kâramanèh's brother Aziz in a cataleptic trance. They are finally revived by injections of a specific called the Golden Elixir—a few drops of which I myself could have used to advantage at this point—and the story sashays fuzzily into its penultimate phase. Accompanied by a sizable police detail, Smith, Petrie, and a Scotland Yard inspector surprise Fu-Manchu in an opium sleep at his hideout. A denouement seems unavoidable, but if there was one branch of literary hopscotch Rohmer excelled in, it was avoiding denouements. When the three leaders of the party recover consciousness (yes, the indispensable trap door again, now on a wholesale basis), they lie bound and gagged in a subterranean vault, watching their captor sacrifice their subordinates by pelting them with poisonous toadstools. The prose rises to an almost lyrical pitch: "Like powdered snow the white spores fell from the roof, frosting the writhing shapes of the already poisoned men. Before my horrified gaze, *the fungus grew*; it spread from the head to the feet of those it touched; it enveloped them as in glittering shrouds. 'They die like flies!' screamed Fu-Manchu, with a sudden febrile excitement; and I felt assured of something I had long suspected: that that magnificent, perverted brain was the brain of a homicidal maniac—though Smith would never accept the theory." Since no hint is given of what theory Smith preferred, we have to fall back on conjecture. More than likely, he smiled indulgently under his gag and dismissed the whole escapade as the prankishness of a spoiled, self-indulgent child.

The ensuing events, while gaudy, are altogether too labyrinthine to unravel. As a matter of fact they puzzled Rohmer, too. He says helplessly, "Any curiosity with which this narrative may leave the reader burdened is shared by the writer." After reading that, my curiosity shrank to the vanishing point; I certainly wasn't going to beat my brains out over a riddle the author himself did not pretend to understand. With a superhuman effort, I rallied just enough inquisitiveness to turn to the last page for some clue to Fu-Manchu's end. It takes place, as nearly as I could gather, in a blazing cottage outside London, and the note he addresses to his antagonists clears the way for plenty of sequels. "To Mr. Commissioner Nayland Smith and Dr. Petrie—Greeting! I am recalled home by One who may not be denied. In much that I came to do I have failed. Much that I have done I would undo; some little I have undone. Out of fire I came—the smoldering fire of a thing one day to be a consuming flame; in fire I go. Seek not my ashes. I am the lord of the fires! Farewell. Fu-Manchu."

I daresay it was the combination of this passage, the cheery hearth in front of which I reread it, and my underwrought condition, but I thought I detected in the Doctor's valedictory an unmistakable mandate. Rising stealthily, I tiptoed up to my daughter's bedchamber and peered in. A shaft of moonlight picked out her ankles protruding from beneath the bed, where she lay peacefully sleeping, secure from dacoity and Thuggee. Obviously, it would take more than a little crackle of the flames below to arouse her.

I slipped downstairs and, loosening the binding of *The Mystery of Dr. Fu-Manchu* to insure a good supply of oxygen, consigned the lord of the fires to his native element. As he crumbled into ash, I could have sworn I smelled a rather rare essential oil and felt a pair of baleful green eyes fixed on me from the staircase. It was probably the cat, though I really didn't take the trouble to check. I just strolled into the kitchen, made sure there was no trap door under the icebox, and curled up for the night. That's how phlegmatic a chap gets in later life.

Rock-a-Bye, Viscount, in the Treetop

A COUPLE of months back, the firm of Bramhall & Rixey, Ltd., a shipping concern on lower Broadway operating a string of freighters to West African ports, received an unusual communication. It was inscribed in pencil on both sides of a sheet of lined yellow paper of the sort commonly employed in secondary schools, and its numerous erasures and interlineations attested to the care that had gone into its composition. The correspondent identified himself as a prominent New York sportsman and big-game hunter who was contemplating a safari into the heart of the Dark Continent (Africa, he explained in a helpful aside). Without going into wearisome detail, he was in a position to assure Bramhall & Rixey that the expedition would eclipse anything of the kind on record. Not only was he planning to bring back a number of leopards, man-eating lions, and comparably gaudy fauna but, if time allowed, he proposed to search out King Solomon's mines and corroborate the existence of a mysterious white goddess ruling a vast empire of blacks in the Cameroons. Obviously, any wide-awake shipping company could appreciate what enormous publicity must accrue to it if chosen to transport such an enterprise.

Should Bramhall & Rixey agree to carry the party—without charge, of course—the sportsman thought he might prevail on his associates to assent, though he warned that they rather favored a rival fleet. Stressing the need for an immediate decision, due to the impending monsoon rains (whether in Manhattan or Africa he did not specify), the writer enclosed a self-addressed postal for a speedy reply.

My first reaction when I came across a postal in my morning mail several days ago with the terse admonition "Wipe your nose, bub," signed by Bramhall & Rixey, was one of spontaneous irritation. I caught up the phone, forgetting for the moment that my fourteen-year-old son had been enthralled this past summer by a book called *Tarzan of the Apes* and that he had been treating the family to a sustained panegyric on Africa. "I'll teach you whose nose to wipe!" I shouted into it. "I've half a mind to come down and cane you people publicly in Beaver Street!" Fortunately, they were spared the humiliation, as, in my wrath, I forgot to dial their number, and by the time I tumbled to the probable culprit and documented his guilt, I was able to take a much more lenient view of the incident. The fact of the matter is that back in 1918, the year I myself first encountered Edgar Rice Burroughs' electrifying fable, it exercised a similarly hypnotic effect on me. Insofar as the topography of Rhode Island and my physique permitted, I modeled myself so closely on Tarzan that I drove the community to the brink of collapse. I flung spears at the neighbors' laundry, exacerbated their watchdogs, swung around their piazzas gibbering and thumping my chest, made reply only in half-human grunts interspersed with unearthly howls, and took great pains generally to qualify as a stench in the civic nostril. The hallucination passed as abruptly as it had set in; one morning I awoke with an overwhelming ennui for everything related to Africa, weak but lucid. My kinsfolk were distrustful for a while, but as soon as they saw me constructing a catamaran in which to explore the Everglades, they knew I was rational again.

Curious as to why Tarzan had enraptured two generations and begotten so many sequels, movie serials, and comics, I commandeered my son's copy of the novel and my wife's chaise longue and staged a reunion. Like most sentimental excursions into the past, it was faintly tinged with disillusion. Across the decades, Burroughs' erstwhile jaunty narrative had developed countless crow's-feet and wrinkles; passages that I remembered outracing Barney Oldfield now seemed to puff and wheeze like a donkey engine. The comparison was aided by a donkey engine puffing directly outside my window, and frequently, in all honesty, its rhythmic snoring was amplified by my own. Nevertheless, I got the gist of the story, and for gist-lovers who prefer to sniff the candy at long range, that little may suffice.

Strictly speaking, the tale begins in the African forest with the adoption by a female anthropoid ape of an English baby of lofty lineage, but to render this association feasible, if not palatable, some valiant exposition is required. Lord and Lady Greystoke, outward bound on the barkentine *Fuwalda* from Freetown in the summer of 1888, are en route "to make a peculiarly delicate investigation of conditions" in a British West Coast colony when mutiny breaks out among the crew. Considering that the captain and his mates are forever emptying revolvers into the men and felling them with belaying pins, Burroughs' appraisal of the situation is dazzlingly understated: "There was in the whole atmosphere of the craft that undefinable something which presages disaster." The lid ultimately blows off, and a lamentable scene ensues: "Both sides were cursing and swearing in a frightful manner, which, together with the reports of the firearms and the screams and groans of the wounded, turned the deck of the *Fuwalda* to the likeness of a madhouse." Lord Greystoke, however, behaves with the coolness one expects of a British peer; through it all, he "stood leaning carelessly beside the companionway puffing meditatively upon his pipe as though he had been but watching an indifferent cricket match." After the mutineers have disposed of authority, the fate of the couple trembles briefly in the balance. Then Black Michael, the ringleader, intercedes for them and persuades his colleagues to maroon the Greystokes in a secluded spot. The speech transmitting this decision somehow recalls the rhetoric of Gilbert and Sullivan's magnanimous scalawags. "You may be all right," he explains kindly, "but it would be a hard matter to land you in civilization without a lot o' questions being asked, and none o' us here has any very convincin' answers up our sleeves."

To skim over the rest of the prologue, the blue bloods survive the immediate rigors of life in the bush; Greystoke, exhibiting a virtuosity rarely met with in castaways and almost never in the House of Lords, builds a stuccoed log cabin furnished with cozy appurtenances like bamboo curtains and bookcases, and his wife, materially aiding the story line, presents him with a male child. But all unbeknownst to the patrician pair, their hourglass is already running out. Her Ladyship, badly frightened by a marauding ape, expires on the boy's first birthday, and as her husband sits stricken at the deathbed, a band of apes bent on stealing his rifle invade the cabin and kill him. Among them is Kala, a female whose own babe has just been destroyed by the king of the tribe.

Obeying what Burroughs reverently terms "the call of universal motherhood within her wild breast," and the even greater urgency for a gimmick to set the narrative rolling, she snatches up the English tot, deposits her lifeless one in its cradle, and streaks into the greenery. The blueprint is now technically complete, but the author, ever a man to juggle complications, contrives an extra, masterly touch. Since the cabin contains the schoolbooks from which the lad will learn to read eventually, as well as his father's diary—capriciously written in French—proving his identity, it must be preserved intact. The king ape, therefore, accidentally discharges Greystoke's gun and, fleeing in terror, slams the door shut. Burroughs may foozle his prose on occasion, but when it comes to mortising a plot, he is Foxy Grandpa himself.

It would serve no useful purpose to retrace the arduous youth-hood and adolescence of Tarzan (whose name, incidentally, means "White-Skin," there being no equivalent for Greystoke in ape language), his sanguinary triumphs over a long roster of enemies like leopards, pythons, and boars, and his easy emergence as undisputed boss of the jungle. Superior heredity, of course, gives "the aristocratic scion of an old English house" a vast edge over his primitive associates. Thanks to the invaluable schoolbooks in the cabin, he instinctively learns to read and write—not without hardship, for, says Burroughs, "of the meaning and use of the articles and conjunctions, verbs and adverbs and pronouns, he had but the faintest and haziest conception." But he perseveres, and along with literacy come further civilized attributes. He bathes assiduously, covers his nakedness with pelts, and, out of some dim recess of his consciousness, produces a really definitive method of distinguishing himself from brute creation: "Almost daily, he whetted his keen knife and scraped and whittled at his young beard to eradicate this degrading emblem of apehood. And so he learned to shave—rudely and painfully, it is true—but, nevertheless, effectively." No reasonably astute reader needs to be told twice that when the hero of a popular novel, whether he is Willie Baxter or an ape man, starts shaving, a pair of mischievous blue eyes are right around the corner. However astute, though, no reader could possibly anticipate a simp of the proportions of Jane Porter, or the quartet of frowzy vaudeville stereotypes that now bumble into the picture.

The newcomers, it appears, are a party of treasure-seekers hailing from Baltimore, headed by an absent-minded pedagogue called Professor Archimedes Q. Porter, complete with frock coat and shiny plug hat. In his retinue are Samuel T. Philander, an elderly fusspot secretary straight from the pages of *Puck*; Esmeralda, a corpulent Negro maid aquiver with fear and malapropisms; his daughter Jane, whose beauty ravishes the senses; and, finally, Charley-horsing the long arm of coincidence, Tarzan's own cousin and the incumbent Lord Greystoke, William Cecil Clayton. They, too, have just been involved in a ship's mutiny—Burroughs' favorite literary calamity, evidently—and are now marooned in Tarzan's very parish. Using these piquant ingredients for all they are worth, the author hereupon proceeds to stir up the most delirious chowder of larceny, homicide, aboriginal passion, and haphazard skulduggery ever assembled outside the Newgate calendar. In all this, Tarzan plays the role of the Admirable Crichton, snatching each of the characters, in turn, from the jaws of death and, inevitably, turning Jane Porter's head. The section in which she betrays her partiality for him is sheer poetry. Tarzan is putting the kayo on Terkoz, a bull ape who has abducted Jane: "As the great muscles of the man's back and shoulders knotted beneath the tension of his efforts, and the huge biceps and forearm held at bay those mighty tusks, the veil of centuries of civilization and culture was swept from the blurred vision of the Baltimore girl. When the long knife drank deep a dozen times of Terkoz's heart's blood, and the great carcass rolled lifeless upon the ground, it was a primeval woman who sprang forward with outstretched arms toward the primeval man who had fought for her and won her. And Tarzan? He did what no red-blooded man needs lessons in doing. He took his woman in his arms and smothered her upturned, panting lips with kisses. For a moment Jane Porter lay there with half-closed eyes. . . . But as suddenly as the veil had been withdrawn it dropped again, and an outraged conscience suffused her face with its scarlet mantle, and a mortified woman thrust Tarzan of the Apes from her and buried her face in her hands. . . . She turned upon him like a tigress, striking his great breast with her tiny hands. Tarzan could not understand it." If Tarzan, who was so intimately involved, was baffled, you can imagine my own bewilderment, especially with a donkey engine puffing in my ear. Had the yarn not been so compelling and the chaise longue so comfortable, I would have abandoned both, bearded the Baltimore Chamber of Commerce, and given them my opinion of such a heartless flirt.

While one properly expects major characters as vital as Tarzan and Jane to dominate the canvas, it would be grossly unfair to ignore the figures in the background. Professor Archimedes Q. Porter and his secretary carry the burden of the comic relief, and their sidesplitting misadventures evoke chuckles galore. Herewith, for example, is the Professor's tart rejoinder when Philander nervously informs him they are being stalked by a lion: "'Tut, tut, Mr. Philander,' he chided. 'How often must I ask you to seek that absolute concentration of your mental faculties which alone may permit you to bring to bear the highest powers of intellectuality upon the momentous problems which naturally fall to the lot of great minds? And now I find you guilty of a most flagrant breach of courtesy in interrupting my learned discourse to call attention to a mere quadruped of the genus *Felis*. . . . Never, Mr. Philander, never before have I known one of these animals to be permitted to roam at large from its cage. I shall most certainly report this outrageous breach of ethics to the directors of the adjacent zoological garden.'" Can you tie that? The poor boob's so absent-minded he doesn't even realize he's in *Africa*. An equally rich humorous conceit is Esmeralda, the maid, who is constantly "disgranulated" by all the "gorilephants" and "hipponocerouses" about her. I doubt if Amos 'n' Andy at their most inventive have ever surpassed her attempt to soothe Jane at a moment of crisis: "Yas'm, honey, now you-all go right to sleep. Yo' nerves am all on aidge. What wif all dese ripotamuses and man eaten geniuses dat Marse Philander been a-tellin' about—laws, it ain't no wonder we all get nervous prosecution."

Indeed it ain't, and while the subject of nerves is on the tapis, I suspect that at this point in the action Burroughs himself became a trifle discombobulated. With two-thirds of the piece behind him, he still had to unravel Tarzan's complex genealogy, resolve the love story, account for the Professor's treasure (lost and found half a dozen times throughout), and return his puppets intact to everyday life. Accordingly, he introduces a French cruiser to rescue the Baltimoreans and Clayton, and, once they are safely over the horizon, begins untangling the labyrinthine threads that remain. An officer of the vessel, one D'Arnot, has fallen into the clutches of some local cannibals; Tarzan saves the captive and, in return, is taught French, an accomplishment that enables him to translate his father's diary and legally prove himself the real Lord Greystoke. Armed with the proofs, he hurries to America to claim his mate, but Burroughs is just ahead of him, piling up barriers faster than Tarzan can surmount them. Before he can clasp Jane in his arms, he is compelled to rescue her from a Wisconsin forest fire and eliminate her current fiancé, a Scrooge who financed her father's expedition. The minor matter of the treasure is washed up with a check for two hundred and forty-one thousand dollars, which, the ape man fluently explains to Professor Porter, is its market value. And then, as the lovers' last obstacle vanishes, the author, consummate magician that he is, yanks a final bunny from his hat. Jane jilts Tarzan for his cousin, William Cecil Clayton, and Tarzan, placing her happiness above all, deliberately conceals his true identity. There may be scenes of self-renunciation in Tolstoy that lacerate the heart, but none, I contend, as devastatingly bittersweet as the closing one between the two Greystoke cousins: "'I say, old man,' cried Clayton. 'I haven't had a chance to thank you for all you've done for us. It seems as though you had your hands full saving our lives in Africa and here. . . . We must get better acquainted. . . . If it's any of my business, how the devil did you ever get into that bally jungle?' 'I was born there,' said Tarzan quietly. 'My mother was an Ape, and of course, she couldn't tell me much about it. I never knew who my father was.'"

Ordinarily, my fleeting sojourn in such an equatorial mishmash might have had no worse consequences than myopia and a pronounced revulsion from all noble savages thereafter. As luck would have it, though, the Venetian blind above me slipped its moorings as I finished the romance, and, doubtless overstimulated by Tarzan's gymnastics, I climbed up to restore it. Halfway through the process, the cornice gave way and I was left hanging by my fingernails from the picture molding that encircles the room. At this juncture, a certain fourteen-year-old busybody, who has no better means of employing his time than sending postals to shipowners, came snooping into the room. His pitiless gaze traveled slowly from my pendant form to his copy of *Tarzan of the Apes*. "Watch out, Buster, you'll strain your milk!" he cautioned. "Better leave that stuff to Weissmuller." Yes, sir, it's pretty disheartening. You lie on your back all day worrying about the junk your children read, you hang from moldings, and that's the thanks you get. It's regusting.

Four-and-Twenty Blackjacks

THE MINUTES of the Oxford Union for 1920—a copy of which is, of course, readily available at everyone's elbow—reveal that during its entire winter session that world-famed discussion group and conventicle of pundits was sunk in a mood of almost suicidal despair. The honourable members, thitherto scornful of American eloquence, had become so alarmed at the rhetoric stemming from the Classical High School Debating Society in Providence, Rhode Island, that they were seriously considering mass hara-kiri. "What is the sense of we tongue-tied slobs beating our gums," lamented one Balliol man, summing up the universal sentiment, "when these brilliant Yank speechifiers in faraway New England, every man jack of them a Cicero or Demosthenes, has made a chump out of us oratory-wise?" His defeatism was well grounded; week after week, in a series of dazzling intramural debates, the Rhode Island striplings were exhibiting a fluency rivalling that of Edmund Burke and the elder Pitt on such varied topics as "Resolved: That the Philippines Be Given Their Independence," "Resolved: That the End Justifies the Means," and "Resolved: That the Pen Is Mightier Than the Sword." It was a great natural phenomenon, as inexplicable as parthenogenesis or the strapless bra, and I still feel cocky that I should have presided over it as chairman of the society—well, chairman pro tem, which is almost the same thing. The descendants of Roger Williams don't go in for lousy little distinctions.

The club met every Wednesday afternoon in a classroom that generations of adolescent males had endowed with the reek of a pony stable. It shied a few erasers about to insure a proper concentration of chalk dust in the lungs, and then, as an apéritif to the polemics, listened to an original paper read by one of the membership. Most of these treatises were on fairly cosmic themes; I myself contributed a philippic entitled "Science vs. Religion," an indigestible hash of Robert Ingersoll and Haldeman-Julius, in which I excoriated the Vatican and charged it, under pain of my displeasure, to mend its ways before our next meeting. Occasionally, somebody would alter the pattern and deliver an essay in lighter vein, on, say, "The Witchery of Jack Frost" or "Squeteague Fishing."

Though parliamentary procedure was mother's milk to me, and it was self-evident that I was marked out for political leadership, an altogether fortuitous circumstance scotched my career. One afternoon, while refereeing a tedious forensic battle on the single tax, I somehow lost the thread and became absorbed in a book about a gentleman cracksman called *The Adventures of Jimmie Dale*, by Frank L. Packard. To this day, I cannot account for my psychological brownout; I assume it sprang from the heavy burden of administrative anxieties I was carrying. At any rate, enthralled with the melodrama, I did not discover that the meeting had adjourned until I found Mr. Bludyer, the principal, shaking me violently. He told me that various restoratives, among them my own gavel, had been tried on me without effect and that finally I had been cashiered. "I'd take up some pastime that doesn't tax the intellect, like volleyball," he suggested pointedly. That I went on to score notable gridiron successes and overnight became the idol of the school is unimportant. It was only when the B. M. C. Durfee High School, of Fall River, kayoed us on the issue "Resolved: That Cigarette Smoking Is Injurious to Our Youth" that my rueful colleagues realized the price they had paid for their inconstancy.

Quite recently, at Kaliski & Gabay's auction parlors, I was whipsawed into buying Packard's fable as part of a job lot of second-hand books, and, faced with the dilemma of rereading it or being certified as a spendthrift incapable of handling his own funds, I chose the coward's way. Before I could get into the story, though, I was sidetracked by the publisher's advertisement in the fly-leaves, a sample of the quaint propaganda used in 1917 to popularize the habit of reading. There was nothing like reading, affirmed the A. L. Burt Company, "for a hardworking man, after his daily toil, or in its intervals. It calls for no bodily exertion." The statement may have been true of the four hundred titles that followed, but not of *The Adventures of Jimmie Dale*. Its previous owner had apparently read it while sipping mucilage, for whole episodes were gummed together in the most repulsive fashion. Between prying them apart with a fruit knife, geeing up the fragments, and retrieving the book from the wastebasket, into which it unaccountably kept sliding like a greased pig, I was almost as pooped as the time I whitewashed a three-room henhouse singlehanded.

To anyone who has ever worked his way out of a boxwood maze, the plot of Packard's novel offers no problem, but a supply of pine-knot torches, pickaxes, and shredded paper are indispensable kit for the tyro reader. Each of the two central characters, for example—Jimmie Dale and Marie LaSalle—has three distinct identities. Jimmie is a young millionaire bachelor, an elusive safecracker known as the Gray Seal, and a derelict hophead called Larry the Bat; Marie, likewise rich and socially élite (though forced into hiding by malefactors who crave her money), poses sometimes as the Tocsin, a shadowy fingerwoman, and again as Silver Mag, a disreputable old crone. The lives of the pair—or, more precisely, the six—are forever being sought by scores of hoodlums, gunsels, informers, shyster lawyers, and crooked shamuses, so that they are constantly compelled to switch roles. The upshot is that you are never very positive who is assaulting whom; once or twice, I got the panicky impression that Jimmie's alter egos were throttling each other. This imaginative twist, somewhat akin to the old vaudeville specialty of Desiretta, the Man Who Wrestles with Himself, proved erroneous when I checked up. It was just a couple of other felons.

Obeying the basic canon that romances about gentleman cracksmen begin in ultra-exclusive clubs, *The Adventures of Jimmie Dale* begins in one called the St. James and omits no traditional touch. Herman Carruthers, crusading young editor of the *News-Argus*, is dealing out the usual expository flapdoodle about the Gray Seal ("the kingpin of them all, the most puzzling, bewildering, delightful crook in the annals of crime") to Jimmie, who is so bland, quizzical, and mocking that even the busboys must be aware he is the marauder himself. His blandness grows practically intolerable when Carruthers avers that the kingpin is dead, for, as he and any five-year-old criminologist know, the kingpin is merely dormant until society needs his philanthropic assist. The summons reaches Jimmie that very midnight, at his luxurious

Riverside Drive mansion, in the form of a note from the mysterious feminine mastermind he has never seen, who directs all his exploits. With a curious, cryptic smile tingeing his lips, Jimmie opens his safe and removes exactly what you would expect: "It was not an ordinary belt; it was full of stout-sewn, upright little pockets all the way around, and in the pockets grimly lay an array of fine, blued-steel, highly tempered instruments—a compact, powerful burglar's kit." Half an hour later, an inconspicuous figure flits downtown via Washington Square. Except for the black silk mask, the slouch hat pulled well down over the eyes, and the automatic revolver and electric flashlight, nobody would ever suspect him of being a Raffles.

The actual caper Jimmie executes is too intricate and inconsequential to warrant recapitulating; briefly, by leaving his telltale Gray Seal on a rifled safe, he saves from prison a character who, in behalf of his ailing wife, has heisted his employer's funds. A civic uproar ensues: "The Morning *News-Argus* offered twenty-five thousand dollars reward for the capture of the Gray Seal! Other papers immediately followed suit in varying amounts. The authorities, State and municipal, goaded to desperation, did likewise, and the five million men, women, and children of New York were automatically metamorphosed into embryonic sleuths. New York was aroused." It seems odd that such a *brouhaha* should attend a misdemeanor approximately as monstrous as spitting in the subway, but, no doubt, Manhattan was more strait-laced in that epoch. On the heels of the foregoing comes another sensation—the body of a stool pigeon with alleged evidence linking his murder to the Gray Seal. Our hero's every sensibility is outraged: "Anger, merciless and unrestrained, surged over Jimmie Dale. . . . Even worse to Jimmie Dale's artistic and sensitive temperament was the vilification, the holding up to loathing, contumely, and abhorrence of the name, the stainless name, of the Gray Seal. It *was* stainless! He had guarded it jealously—as a man guards the woman's name he loves." Eyes flashing like cut-steel buckles, he retires to the slum hideout he calls the Sanctuary and revamps himself into Larry the Bat: "His fingers worked quickly—a little wax behind the ears, in the nostrils, under the upper lip, deftly placed—hands, wrists, neck, throat, and face received their quota of stain, applied with an artist's touch—and then the spruce, muscular Jimmie Dale, transformed into a slouching, vicious-featured denizen of the underworld, replaced the box under the flooring, pulled a slouch hat over his eyes, extinguished the gas, and went out." By dint of certain devious researches, which I could not extricate from the glue, a venal police inspector is unmasked as the culprit and the Gray Seal absolved. If my calculations are correct, Jimmie in the first sixty pages of the action has enjoyed a grand total of eleven minutes sleep, considerably less than the most wide-awake reader.

Stimulated to a healthy glow by these finger exercises, Jimmie now dashes off an ambitious four-part fugue plangent with larceny and homicide. Under the pretense of glomming a diamond chaplet from the strongbox of a rascally broker, he recovers a note held by the Scrooge against a mining engineer he has fleeced, bilks a ring of counterfeiters blackmailing a sheep in their toils, robs a dealer of gems to obviate his being slaughtered by yeggs (a curious bit of preventive surgery), and exposes a knavish banker named Carling who has looted his own vaults and pinned the blame on an underling with a criminal record. In the last-named coup, the accused has a winsome infant, enabling Packard to pull out the vox-humana stop when Jimmie extorts the vital confession: "'Carling,' said Jimmie hoarsely, 'I stood beside a little bed tonight and looked at a baby girl—a little baby girl with golden hair, who smiled as she slept. . . . Take this pen, or—this.' The automatic lifted until the muzzle was on a line with Carling's eyes." Jimmie's antisocial behavior, it goes without saying, never redounds to his personal advantage; he scrupulously returns all swag to its rightful owners and, even while bashing in whatever skulls deserve it, exudes the high moral purpose of his progenitor Robin Hood. True, he betrays a pallid romantic interest in the Maid Marian who animates him from behind the scenes, but nothing that would boil an egg. In the light of contemporary pulp fiction, one marvels that Packard spiced his famous goulash with so little sexual paprika. Perhaps it may be possible to sublimate the libido by twiddling the combination of a Herring-Hall-Marvin safe, or, on the other hand, perhaps the kid's just a medical curiosity. Nobody could be *that* dedicated.

And yet he is, unless you discount the evidence of the next hundred pages. In rapid succession, he clears the reputation of a putative ruby thief, brings to book the architect of a payroll killing and his henchmen, and restores the stolen map of a gold mine to the widow and children of its legal claimant. There is a magnificent consistency about Packard's minor figures; other writers may muck about with halftones and nuances, but his widows are all destitute and enfeebled and his villains are rotten to the core. A typical sample is the satanic attorney who conceived the payroll incident above: "Cunning, shrewd, crafty, conscienceless, cold-blooded—that was Stangeist . . . the six-foot muscular frame, that was invariably clothed in attire of the most fashionable cut; the thin lips with their oily, plausible smile, the straight black hair that straggled into pinpoint, little black eyes, the dark face with its high cheekbones, which, with the pronounced aquiline nose and the persistent rumor that he was a quarter caste, had led the underworld, prejudiced always in favor of a 'monaker,' to dub the man the 'Indian Chief.'" A Choctaw version of Louis Calhern in *The Asphalt Jungle*, you might say, and a real ripsnorter. The argot in which the crooks converse also has the same classical purity; *vide* that of the Weasel, an obscure cutpurse who stirs recollections of Happy Hooligan, of sainted memory: "Why, youse damned fool," jeered the Weasel, "d'youse t'ink youse can get away wid dat? Say, take it from me, youse are a piker! Say, youse make me tired. Wot d'youse t'ink youse are? D'youse t'ink dis is a tee-ayter, an' dat youse are a cheap-skate actor strollin' acrost the stage?" Scant wonder, with such nostalgic Chimmie Fadden dialogue, that youse has to swallow repeatedly to exorcise de lump in de t'roat.

The machine-gun tempo, to use a flabby designation, slackens momentarily for an interview in the dark between Jimmie and the Tocsin, his female control. His work is nearing completion, she whispers, and soon she can disclose herself with impunity. This, as the intuitive will guess, is the conventional literary strip tease, because in the next breath the deluge descends. The Crime Club—not the Doubleday fellows, but "the most powerful and pitiless organization of criminals the world has ever known"—pounces on the dapper thief. In a scary milieu replete with hydraulic walls, sliding laboratories, and a binful of putty noses and false whiskers, its minions vainly ply him with a truth drug to elicit word of the Tocsin's whereabouts. No contusions result, except to the laws of English syntax, and Jimmie is let out to pasture. It would only court neuralgia to retrace the labyrinthine steps by which the author maneuvers him into the arms of his lady, now disguised as Silver Mag, the beggarwoman, but ultimately the lovebirds make contact and the lava spills over: "The warm, rich lips were yielding to his; he could feel that throb, the life in the young, lithe form against his own. She was his—his! The years, the past, all were swept away—and she was his at last—his for always. And there came a mighty sense of kingship upon him, as though all the world were at his feet, and virility, and a great, glad strength above all other men's, and a song was in his soul, a song triumphant—for she was his!" In other words, she was his, *Gott sei dank*, and you have just burst into sobs of relief when the whole confounded business begins over again. Marie LaSalle, alias the Tocsin, alias Silver Mag, pours out a long, garbled *histoire*, the kernel of which is that the head of the Crime Club, posing as her uncle, seeks to kill her for her estate. Jimmie manages to worm a confession from him clinching his guilt; in the attendant melee, though, he is recognized as the Gray Seal, and a wrathful mob of vigilantes from the Tenderloin tracks him to the Sanctuary and puts it to the torch. The lovers providentially escape over the rooftops to continue their didos in *The Further Adventures of Jimmie Dale*, *Jimmie Dale and the Phantom Clue*, and *Jimmie Dale and the Blue Envelope*, and blessed silence descends, broken only by the scratch of Packard's pen endorsing his royalty checks.

I was in a Sixth Avenue bus, traffic-bound in Herald Square, when I finished the last three chapters, and a natural impulse to break clean made me drop the book into the vacant seat before me. Moments later, a brace of speedy sixteen-year-olds in windbreakers emblazoned with side elevations of Jane Russell crash-dived into the seat and buried themselves in comics. One of them suddenly detected the volume nestling against his spine. "Hey!" he exclaimed. "Someone lost a book." "It ain't a book. There's no pictures in it," his companion corrected. Together they laboriously spelled out the title and joined in a quick, incurious survey of the contents. "Ah, just a lot of slush," observed the first, in disdain. "What kind of an old creep'd get a charge out of this stuff?" An old creep directly behind them turned blush-pink, fastened his eyes on a Mojud stocking ad, and strove to retain his dignity. At Forty-second Street, weary of their tiresome speculation and guffaws, he disembarked, not, however, without a shrivelling glance. If you ask me, popinjays like that, and all these young whippersnappers you meet nowadays, have no more character than a tin pie plate. Why, at their age I was already chairman of a world-famed debating society.

Oh, Sing Again That
Song of Venery

BACK in the spring of 1926, that idyllic period which now seems
to have been part of the Golden Age, there throve midway along
West Eighth Street, in Greenwich Village, a restaurant known as
Alice McCollister's. It had a pleasant back-yard garden, where
tweedy, artistic folk were wont to breakfast on Sunday morn-
ings, equably discussing such avant-gardist tendencies as Fouji-
ta's painting, the novels of Floyd Dell, and the composographs of
Peaches Browning. Every once in a while, the Sabbath peace veil-
ing the premises would be fractured by a piercing clarinet arpeg-
gio from above, and, looking up in irritation, the patrons would
perceive a strange figure seated on the fourth-floor window sill
of an adjoining building. His gaunt face was strikingly similar to
that of George Arliss, an illusion he fostered by affecting the sort
of monocle worn by the star of *The Green Goddess*. His hair, luxuriant as a fat-tailed sheep's, hung low on his neck, and the visible
portion of his body was clad in a Russian tunic decorated with
red and blue cross-stitch. Braced in the window frame, his licorice
stick wailing forth a freehand version of "Milenberg Joys," Hilary Tremayne would be notifying the world in his usual heterodox

fashion that he was a free spirit. He would also be giving his three roommates, of whom I was the sleepiest, a persistent pain in the fundament.

Considering that we all shared a chamber roughly seventeen by twelve for six months, I knew relatively little about Hilary, but what little I knew was enough. An actor by profession, he had early adopted the name of Tremayne as a stylish variant of his own, which was, I believe, either Troutman or Appenzeller. His major acting triumphs had occurred south of Fourteenth Street, in Restoration comedies at the Cherry Lane, though on one occasion he had impersonated a faun in the Theatre Guild production of Franz Werfel's *Goat Song.* Currently, he was attending Richard Boleslavsky's school of the drama, and he was forever using terms like "dynamics," "spatial interplay," and "Aristotelian progression" to explain what went on behind the footlights. Guilfoyle and Froelich, the two other roommates, were the only members of our quartet with any semblance of a steady income. The former, a neat, bloodless youth, worked as bookkeeper at a stevedoring concern down around Bowling Green. He was engaged to a deeply devout girl in Brooklyn who disapproved of his bohemian associates, and, when he was not escorting her to vespers, which was seldom indeed, hovered before the mirror searching his alabaster skin for blemishes. Froelich, a salesman for household appliances and the Don Juan of the fraternity, was no older than the rest of us, but his excursions into a thousand boudoirs had given him a premature suavity and polish that, as he freely admitted, turned women's bones to water at a single glance. Ninety per cent of the incoming calls on our telephone were beamed at Froelich—lovelorn wives whose husbands were away on business trips and who thirsted for his ministrations, he said, with a self-deprecatory shrug, and patted his receding hairline. I often wondered why he stayed in the Village, since, like Guilfoyle's fiancée, he professed intense scorn for its crackpot literati and painters. One day, he enlightened me. He hoped to compose popular songs eventually, and felt he owed it to his muse to steep himself in a milieu charged with significant new rhythms. "Besides," he added pensively, "there's a lot of gorgeous quail in this section."

Wave on wave of such Proustian memories—well, if not waves, a needle shower—buffeted me the other day when, cropping through a Pennsylvania country library, I came across a copy of a book called *Leonie of the Jungle*, by Joan Conquest. Miss Conquest's novel was one item of my spiritual pabulum in that remote era—the roast course, you might say. I read it at Froelich's recommendation (his literary taste was as catholic as his choice of bedfellows), and if it did nothing else, it at least spared me the expense of an electric heater those chilly spring evenings. Though I had long ago forgotten the background, characters, and plot, I distinctly remembered it as a lollapaloosa; even plucking the volume from the shelf produced a vague incandescence in my cheeks, comparable to the effect of a double Chartreuse. I stole a sidelong look at the librarian, nodding over her rubber stamps, and, with a quick, shoplifter's gesture, whipped it under my mackinaw. Whether it was guilt that made my heart pound all the way home or the evocative powers of the book, I cannot say for certain, but by the time I reached my own rooftree, I was in a lather of perspiration.

It began to dawn on me shortly after rereading a few pages that my crime was doubly heinous in that I had mulcted an object of no value whatever; far from robbing the library, in fact, I had unwittingly done a salutary job of scavenging. Somewhere over the past quarter century, the juice of the novel had calcified, or my nature had so coarsened that it derived very little moxie from the tale of an English girl's enslavement by a sinister Indian sect. Nevertheless, kleptomaniac and boor though I had become, I still had enough decency not to fling it aside with a snap judgment. Lighting up a Murad to induce nostalgia, and greasing my face with butter to protect it from the burning prose, I wallowed into the text like a Channel swimmer leaving Cape Gris-Nez.

The heroine of *Leonie of the Jungle* makes her curtsy to us at the age of seven in a locale largely unexplored in the fiction of the budding twenties—a psychoanalyst's office. An orphan afflicted with somnambulism and malevolent dreams, she has been brought to a Harley Street specialist named Sir Jonathan Cuxson by her aunt, Lady Susan Hetth. Leonie is a veritable dewdrop of a child, with opalescent, gold-flecked eyes and a lisp that would melt the glue out of a revolving bookcase. The mention of a possible jog on a pony, for instance, precipitates the following: "'I can't wide astwide,' she sighed. 'I haven't any bweeches. . . . But I can swim, an' jump in out of my depff. I learnt in the baff at the seaside!'" Inquiries by Sir Jonathan establish that an Indian nurse gained a strong ascendancy over Leonie during her babyhood in India and may even have endowed her with strange psychic potency. The latter supposition is confirmed at the Zoo, to which she is taken by Jan, the Doctor's son; she handles a ravening Bengal tiger at will, doubtless anesthetizing the beast with her dialogue. "'*Poor* tiger!' she was saying. 'I'm vewwy sowwy for you—I'm sure you're not so vewy, vewy wicked, an' if you will bend your head, I will stwoke you behind the ear same as I did Kitty.'" Thanks to a chicken-hearted social system that forbids euthanasia for people who talk this way, Leonie is permitted to grow up and go to boarding school, where she practices sleepwalking almost as intensively as her colleagues do field hockey. In consequence, she is considered rather odd, an estimate that has some physical justification also, for the author says of her hands that "the fingers were like pea-pods, long and slender and slightly dimpled." You could hardly expect anybody, let alone a group of teen-age girls, to warm up to an ambulatory mess of greens drifting around in the moonlight and chanting, "I make oblation . . . let the gods come well willing!" It's vewwy unnerving, reawwy.

Her schooling finished, Leonie settles down on the north Devon coast with her aunt and there is forced into wedding Sir Walter Hickle, a loathsome, baseborn blackmailer who has been preying on Lady Susan. The union is particularly odious because, before it takes place, Leonie has met Jan Cuxson again and fallen in love with him. Jan, now a physician carrying on his father's work, chances to spy her during a somnambulistic sei-zure in which she executes a voluptuous belly dance invoking Kali, the Indian goddess of death. He tries to convince her that she is not daffy, as the evidence would indicate, but simply the victim of long-range mesmerism from India, interlarding the diagnosis with feverish busses and appeals to marry him instead of Sir Walter. That Leonie should mulishly reject his suit when it is open and shut that they are unavoidably headed for the same ostermoor seems a shade quixotic. Still, Miss Conquest has two hundred pages of Oriental monkeyshines to vend, and no paren-thetical smooching is going to upset her applecart. The marriage, therefore, takes place on schedule; Jan, unreconciled, departs for India to track down Leonie's incubus—presumably by advertising in the incubus column of the Bombay *Daily Mail*—and en route receives the cheery news that Sir Walter has perished in a fire on his wedding night. This deft bit of author's convenience effectively preserves the heroine's virginity for the second half of the book, when it will be called upon to weather truly hideous ordeals, and now the real fireworks begin.

The Svengali actually responsible for Leonie's trauma, it appears, is a prince's son named Madhū Krishnaghar, who by sorcery and incantation has been striving to lure her back to the Peninsula to serve as his plaything and as priestess to Kali. His fiendish magic prevails. A few weeks later, we join the bewitched maiden aboard a liner steaming up the Hooghly, sleepwalking thirteen to the dozen. Madhū, a charm boy resembling Ramon Novarro at his prime, has sneaked on at Colombo, and here is the vision he sees as she trips out on deck in her nightgown: "She made an arresting picture as she stood listening intently, her flimsy garment falling away from her shoulders, leaving the slender white back bare to the waist, while she held handfuls of the transparent stuff crushed against her breast, upon which lay a jewel hung from a gold chain. . . . Sweetly she laughed up into his face as she laid one little hand upon the great white cloak which swung from his shoulders, unaware that in moving her hand her own garment had slipped, and that her beauty lay exposed like a lotus bud before his eyes. She came so close that her bare shoulder touched the fine white linen, and the curves of her scarlet lips were but a fraction of an inch from his own; and her whispered words in the eastern tongue were as a flame to an oil well." Even across the gulf of twenty-five years, I can still remember the thread of saliva that coursed down Froelich's chin as he read the foregoing passage aloud to us.

His carnal instincts, I suppose, had been so whetted on importunate housewives that he found the sweetmeat irresistible. Madhū Krishnaghar, while sorely beset, displays greater self-control: "No movement of his body, but he gave a jerk of his willpower which brought the veins out like whipcord on his forehead, and drove the nails deep into the palms of his hands." In this awkward condition, he is plainly in no shape to wreak his will of Leonie, and she disembarks unsullied at Calcutta, blissfully ignorant, like Clarissa Harlowe, that her virtue is about to undergo further titanic stresses.

For a while, all is fun and games. Leonie turns the heads of the local sahibs, who haven't seen a podful of fresh peas since leaving Gib; she comports herself splendidly on a tiger shoot; and she pitches some woo with Dr. Jan, who, of course, behaves with gentlemanly British restraint even though the vapor is whistling from his ears. In a scene where he holds her "crushed to the point of agony against him with his mouth upon the sweetness of her neck," the author grows rather tart because he doesn't assert himself more strongly. "Heavens!" she exclaims. "What fools some men can be with that jungle animal woman within their hands! . . . Good heavens, why didn't he take her in his arms and smother her up against his heart, or put a bag over her head, or failing the bag, put his hand before her eyes?" At any rate, bored with his spineless grazing on her neck and his namby-pamby proposals, Leonie succumbs to the magnetism being exerted on her by Madhū Krishnaghar and takes off on a sightseeing tour of Benares. In the cupola of a temple near the holy city, Madhū, ostensibly acting as her guide, slips her a goof ball that paralyzes her will, and uncorks a plethora of such incendiary phrases as "thou white doe," "thou virgin snow," and so forth. Leonie responds with an abandon that would shame a dish of junket: "Wave after wave swept her from head to foot, causing her body, untrammeled by whalebone, to tremble against his, and he loosened the white cloak and let it fall, holding her pressed to him in her thin silk dress, laughing down at her, delighting in her eyes, her mouth, her throat." Yet before the sparks she has generated can leap into a holocaust, Miss Conquest perversely stamps them out. "He had not the slightest intention of doing her any harm," she notes, pursing her lips into a prim line, "but with the whole of his vividly mature brain and virgin body, he delighted in the effect of the drug upon the woman he loved." In other words, just a fun-loving kid motivated by curiosity, like any adolescent with his first chemistry kit.

The gambol in the cupola, it soon transpires, is merely antipasto for a real shindig at the Praying Ghats, the sacred stairs fronting the Ganges. Here, under the malign influence of Kali, Madhū and Leonie dunk each other in the river, hemstitch their frames with daggers, and generally take advantage of every inch of platitude allowed by the postal laws.

As the pressure intensifies and ecstasy fogs the author's lens, Leonie enters what can only be described as a chronic state of near-ravishment: "Leonie lay still, unconscious of the sound and the subtle change creeping over the man who bent down to her, and who, high-caste, over-educated, overstrung, aflame with love and afire with the sensuality of his religion, slowly tightened his hand upon the gracious curves of the slender throat." This and ancillary didos culminate in a whopper of an orgy at an adjacent temple, from which Leonie is delivered with her camisole in ribbons but her chastity, *Gott sei Dank*, intact. By now, to be excessively blunt, the reader would cheerfully assent to the game's being called on account of darkness, Madhū awarded the trophy on a technicality, and the arena hosed down. Whatever Miss Conquest's deficiencies as a novelist, however, she has one inflexible tenet: She never gives short weight.

Jan Cuxson, we discover in a flashback, has not failed his beloved, and through all her vicissitudes has been hot on her scent. Comparatively hot, that is; at the moment, he lies prisoner, chained to a ring in the wall, in the very temple where Leonie was drugged. His captor is a fanatical old priest who forgets to feed him for days at a time and occasionally spits on him, but, like Madhū, isn't really a bad egg: "The fine old man had no intention of torturing the white man, he had merely bound him to the ring until his goddess should inspire him, her servant, with her wishes." Gramps, as one is tempted to dub him, reveals to Jan that he consecrated Leonie as a baby to the divinity and that she will ultimately fetch up at his altar to be sacrificed. To save excessive travel and assure himself of a ringside seat at the blowoff, Jan sensibly decides to sit tight and await developments. In due time, Madhū and Leonie descend on the district, pale with exertion, but still full of ginger. They have been skittering all over western Bengal, playing puss in the corner and exchanging speeches like "Thy mouth is even as the *bimba* fruit, which is warm and soft, and thy chin is like a mango stone, and thy neck like unto a conch shell which I encircle with both hands." If any prospective Ph.D. longs to investigate the role of the neck in erotic literature, he has a mine of source material in *Leonie of the Jungle*. At all events, Leonie suddenly throws off Madhū's spell, realizes her degradation, and spurns his love; he, incensed, hands her over to the priest, and then, just as she is about to be skewered, relents and averts the sacrificial blade. Simultaneously, Jan bursts his bonds, and the over-wrought author caps her climax with the classic device for finishing any story, "the greatest earthquake that ever swept the Sunderbunds Jungle." Madhū and the priest, quite properly, are expunged—the latter, with true consideration, releasing Leonie from the hex with his dying breath—and the lovers clinch in the afterglow. "There has been a bit of an earthquake, dear," Jan discloses in reply to his affinity's questions, "and you got hit on the head by a piece of falling brick." Leonie, her opalescent, gold-flecked eyes like saucers, demands reassurance: "Where are we going to? Where are you taking me?" "To Devon, beloved," returns Jan, sealing her mouth with honest, Occidental-type kisses. "To Devon and happiness!"

There is an old saying in my part of Pennsylvania, and I wish I could convey its sonorous beauty in Pennsylvania Dutch, that he who filches library books is a *Schwein* and that unto him there will subsequently come a day of reckoning. I never dreamt what wisdom the adage contains or how swiftly vengeance would overtake my transgression. Barely had I lifted my head from the last page of the book when my collar button, released from the tension it had been under for the previous two hours, popped off and struck the reading lamp, shivering it to smithereens. The room was plunged in darkness, and as I sat there, stunned, a low, sepulchral, and extremely horrid voice addressed me. "*Ham abhi ate hai*," it said forebodingly. "*Ham abhi ate hai*." Which, as the least accomplished student of Hindustani knows, means "I come—I come." It might have issued from the Pennsylvania Library Association or from some recondite Indian deity, but I had no overpowering urge to inquire. With a bound, I lit out onto the lawn, where I could have plenty of room to rassle. I caught a hell of a cold, spent three days in bed, and still can't figure out a way to return the book gracefully. Has anybody got a reliable fence? Has anybody got a single suggestion or, for that matter, an iota of pity? Me, I've got nothing—just rhinitis, a first edition of *Leonie of the Jungle*, and a podful of remorse.

When to the Sessions
of Sweet Silent Films . . .

On a slumberous afternoon in the autumn of 1919, the shopkeep-
ers along Weybosset Street in Providence, Rhode Island, were
nonplused by a mysterious blinding flash. Simultaneously, they
heard a sound like a gigantic champagne cork being sucked out of
a bottle, and their windows bulged inward as though Dario Resta's
Peugeot had passed, traveling at incalculable speed. Erupting
from their bazaars, they saw a puny figure streaking in the direction of the Victory, the town's leading cinema. The first report,
that anarchists had blown the cupola off the state capitol, swiftly
yielded to a second, that a gopher mob had knocked over the vault
of the Mercers' & Pursers' Trust Co. Before either rumor could be
checked, a bystander appeared with a green baize bag dropped by
the fugitive, establishing him as a sophomore at the Classical High
School. Among its contents were a copy of Caesar's Gallic commentaries, a half-eaten jelly sandwich, and a newspaper advertisement announcing the première that afternoon at the Victory of
Cecil B. De Mille's newest epic, *Male and Female*, starring Thomas
Meighan, Gloria Swanson, and Lila Lee.

By the time the foregoing had been pieced together, of course, the sophomore in question—whose measurements coincided exactly with my own—was hanging out of a balcony seat at the Victory in a catatonic state, impervious to everything but the photoplay dancing on the screen. My absorption was fortunate, for at regular intervals the ushers circulated through the aisles, spraying the audience with an orange scent that practically ate away the mucous membrane. Whether this was intended to stimulate the libido or inhibit it, I never found out, but twenty years later, when I met Mr. De Mille in Hollywood, I could have sworn he exuded the same fragrance. The fact that we met in an orange grove, while relevant, did not materially alter my conviction.

Male and Female, as moviegoers of that epoch will recall, was based on James M. Barrie's *The Admirable Crichton*, a play that derided caste and sought to demonstrate how a family of *hochgeboren* snobs, marooned on a desert island, was salvaged physically and spiritually by its butler. That so special a problem could enthrall a youth living on a New England chicken farm might seem unlikely, but it did, and to such a degree that I saw the picture twice over again on the spot. The silken luxury of its settings, the worldliness and bon ton of the characters, and their harrowing privations held me spellbound. I was bewitched in particular by the butler as portrayed by Thomas Meighan. His devastating aplomb, the cool, quiet authority with which he administered his island kingdom and subdued the spitfire Lady Mary Lasenby, played by Miss Swanson, displaced every previous matinée idol from my heart. For weeks afterward, while toting mash to the hens or fumigating their perches, I would fall into noble attitudes and apostrophize the flock with lines like "One cannot tell what may be in a man, Milady. If all were to return to Nature tomorrow, the same man might not be master, nor the same man servant.

Shall I serve the ices in the conservatory?" The consequences of this sort of lallygagging soon made themselves felt. There was a sharp decline in egg production, followed almost immediately by word from the Classical High School that I had achieved the lowest grade ever recorded in second-year Latin.

Quite recently, through the good offices of the Museum of Modern Art, I was enabled to re-examine the masterwork that gave me so profound a catharsis. It was a reassuring experience; I discovered that although the world is topsy-turvy, De Mille still remains the same. His latest pictures display the same baroque pomp, the same good old five-cent philosophy, and the same lofty disregard for sense. *Male and Female* could be remade today with equal success at the box office. All I ask in return for the suggestion is that prior to its release I be given twenty-four hours' head start.

The film begins with a pious explanation that its title is derived from the passage in Genesis "Male and female created He them," and first introduces a scullery maid named Tweeny, in the person of Lila Lee. Tweeny is employed at fashionable Loam House, in London, where she nurses a violent, unreciprocated passion for its major-domo, Crichton. We now meet, in a series of keyhole shots, the various members of the Loam family as they appear to an impudent pageboy delivering their boots. They are, respectively, the Earl (Theodore Roberts), his silly-ass cousin Ernest (Raymond Hatton), and his daughters, Lady Mary and Lady Agatha. Miss Swanson, the former, reclines on a couch worthy of the Serpent of the Nile, having her nails and hair done by a pair of maids. This lovely sybarite is to learn, says an acid subtitle, that "hands are not only to be manicured but to work with, heads not only to dress but to think with, hearts not only to beat but to love

with." Her sister, a languid wraith engaged in scrutinizing her cos-
metic mask, fares no more kindly: "Lady Agatha, who is to find
like most beauties that the condition of her face is less important
than to learn to face conditions." There follows a piquant scene
wherein Miss Swanson dons a peekaboo negligee, sinuously peels
to enter a sunken marble tub, and sluices down in a shower containing a spigot marked "Toilet Water." Emerging, she finds a box
of long-stemmed roses sent by an admirer named Lord Brocklehurst. The accompanying card read (as I thought), "My Lady of
the Roses: I am coming over to show you something interesting
for the slim white finger of your slim third hand," but this seemed
so Surrealist in mood that I had the projectionist run it again. The
actual phrase, "slim third finger of your slim white hand," is pretty
humdrum by comparison.

Depicted next is the ritual of Lady Mary's breakfast, served
by three underlings and presided over by Crichton. "The toast
is spoiled," declares his mistress capriciously. "It's entirely too
soft." Ever the flower of courtesy, Crichton pinks her neatly in the
ego with a deadpan riposte: "Are you sure, Milady, that the toast
is the only thing that is spoiled?" Leaving her to gnash her teeth
on the soggy toast, he descends to the library, where Tweeny is
dusting, and proceeds to read aloud, for no cogent reason, a dol-
lop of poesy by William Ernest Henley beginning, "I was a King
in Babylon and you were a Christian slave." The scullery maid,
eyes swimming with adoration, furtively strokes his instep. "I
wouldn't be nobody's slave, I wouldn't," she murmurs. "Unless
maybe your slave." Lady Mary, who by a spooky coincidence has
been reading the very same book earlier, now enters just in time
to hear Crichton declaiming, "I saw, I took, I cast you by, I gently
broke your pride." The delicious spectacle of varlets pretending to

understand poetry evokes her patrician mirth, and, imperiously requisitioning the book, she goes to greet Lord Brocklehurst, her suitor.

Brocklehurst, by and large, is an inconsequential character in the drama—merely a lay figure dragged in to spice the budding romance between Lady Mary and Crichton. The plot, which has been betraying definite symptoms of rigor mortis, comes alive about teatime, when the Loams, frantic with ennui, determine to cruise to the South Seas in their yacht. As they animatedly begin studying maps, a confidante of Lady Mary's, Lady Eileen Duncraigie, drops in to consult her about a glandular dilemma. She is infatuated with her chauffeur—one of those typical crushes that followed in the wake of the internal-combustion engine—and wonders whether she stands any chance of happiness. Lady Mary smiles commiseratingly. Indicating a bird cage nearby, she poses a searching zoological parallel: "Would you put a jackdaw and a bird of paradise in the same cage? It's *kind to kind*, Eileen, and you and I can never change it." Well, sir, you know what happens to people who run off at the mouth like that. It's even money La Belle Swanson will be eating crow before the turn of the monsoon, and the cinematic bobbin shuttles madly back and forth as it starts weaving her comeuppance.

Dissolving to the Loam yacht at sea, we observe our principals leading the same unregenerate existence—squabbling endlessly and being coddled by Crichton, whose insteps, in turn, are being dogged by Tweeny. In a newspaper presumably flown to her by albatross, Lady Mary reads of her friend's marriage to her chauffeur. "I suppose," waggishly remarks Ernest, "that if one married a chauffeur, one would soon *tire* of him—get it?" Lady Mary haughtily rejoins that the whole affair is ridiculous—exactly as if she were to marry Crichton. The latter's face freezes as he overhears the slur, and when Thomas Meighan's face, already icy to begin with, froze, it looked like Christmas at Crawford Notch. "And there," explains a crunchy caption, "it might have ended had they not been blown by the Winds of Chance into uncharted Tropic Seas with Destiny smiling at the wheel." Which, draining away the schmaltz, is to say that the yacht runs aground, the crew obligingly perishes, and the Loams, plus their retinue, are washed up intact. The shot that gave one the old *frisson* in 1919, of course, was Meighan carrying Miss Swanson, more dead than alive and more naked than not, out of the surf. It is still gripping, and for those who are curious about its effect on Meighan—inasmuch as there is no clue to be found in his features—the succeeding title is helpful: "Suddenly, like mist melting before the sun, she was no longer a great lady to him, but just a woman, a very helpless and beautiful woman." Brother, they don't write subtitles like that any more. The fellows who dream up the scenarios nowadays are daffy enough, to be sure, but there's no *poetry* in them.

It takes approximately a reel and a half of celluloid and some of the most cumbersome foolery since the retirement of Louise Fazenda to reunite the shipwrecked party. The Earl, who has landed in a dressing gown and yachting cap, chewing the celebrated Theodore Roberts cigar, becomes embroiled in various comic misadventures, such as nestling against a turtle he mistakes for a boulder and disputing possession of a coconut with some chimpanzees. The mishmash of fauna on the island, by the way, would confound any naturalist past the age of twelve; I doubt whether Alfred Russel Wallace, either in the depths of the Malay Archipelago or malarial fever, ever saw apes and mountain goats, wild boars and leopards, sharing a Pacific atoll. When noses are finally counted, the survivors number seven—the four Loams, Crichton and Tweeny, and an unidentified young minister whose presence is never quite explained but whom De Mille was doubtless limbering up for one of his later Biblical productions. Crichton borrows the padre's watch crystal to light a fire, allots various chores to the group, and in short order manages to arouse Lady Mary's anger. When he proposes to use her gold lace stole as a fish net, she rebels openly and talks the others into seceding, but the revolt soon collapses. One by one, the insurgents sneak back to Crichton's fire and his kettle of seaweed broth, leaving her impenitent and alone. Then she too weakens, for, as the subtitle puts it, "You may resist hunger, you may resist cold, but the fear of the unseen can break the strongest will." The unseen in this case takes the form of a moth-eaten cheetah rented from Charlie Gay's lion farm in El Monte. As he noses through the undergrowth, Lady Mary's nerve cracks and she scurries to Crichton for protection. Ultimately, after much digging of her toe awkwardly in the hot sand, or what used to be known as the Charlie Ray school of acting, she knocks under and ponies up the gold lace stole. The sequence, or the round, or whatever it is, ends with both breathing hard but not the least bit winded—considerably more, goodness knows, than can be said for the spectator.

"Under the whiplash of necessity," the narrative continues sonorously, "they come to find that the wilderness is cruel only to the drone, that her grassy slopes may clothe the ragged, her wild boar feed the hungry, her wild goats slake their thirst." Two years, we discover, have wrought substantial changes in the castaways. They have fashioned themselves a nobby compound, domesticated everything in sight but the chiggers, and dwell contentedly under a benevolent despotism set up by Crichton.

Lady Mary and Lady Agatha, in play suits of woven bark and in Robinson Crusoe hats, skip over the savannas hunting wild fowl with bow and arrow; the Earl, still chewing the same cigar stump, hauls lobster pots on the lagoon; Ernest and the anonymous divine milk goats in a corral; Tweeny, whose status nothing apparently can alter, stirs a caldron of poi in the kitchen; and Crichton, garbed in a tunic resembling a Roman centurion's made of palm fronds, labors in his study on a Boob McNutt contraption designed to ignite a rescue flare on the cliffs. His new eminence is illustrated at mealtime that evening, when he is revealed dining in splendid isolation, fanned by a punkah that is operated by Lady Mary. Henley's poems, providentially saved from the wreck, are propped up before him, and he is rereading "I was a King in Babylon," the eternal references to which were beginning to give me a dull pain in the base of my scullery. It presently develops that the greedy old Earl has eaten some figs earmarked for Crichton's dessert, and Lady Mary hurries to pick more. Learning she has gone to "the drinking place of the leopards," Crichton hastens after her and transfixes one of the beasts as it attacks. She gratefully flings herself into his arms, and confesses her belief that he is the reincarnation of a king in Babylon. "Then you were a Christian slave," he says with sudden understanding, turning her face up to his. The action thereupon pauses for what is unquestionably the snazziest flashback that has ever emerged from silver nitrate. Meighan, duked out as a Semitic tyrant on the order of Ashurbanipal, receives from a vassal a tigerish, scantily clad slave girl—i.e., Miss Swanson—who repays his tentative caresses by biting him in the wrist. With a cruel sneer, he promises to tame her, and she is borne off snarling defiance in the classic tradition. In due time, she re-enters on a palanquin powered by Nubians, clothed in sequins and wearing on her head a triumph of the taxidermist's art, a stuffed white peacock. "Bring forth the sacred lions of Ishtar," Meighan commands, gesturing toward an arena installed meanwhile by the studio carpenters. "Choose thine own fate. Yield to me willingly or thou shalt know the fitting cage built for thee, O Tiger Woman." Secure in her long-term contract, Miss Swanson proudly elevates her chin. "Through lives and lives you shall pay, O King," she predicts, and advances into the pit. As the episode concludes, we are back on the island, with Crichton telling Lady Mary, in mettlesome spondees, "I know I've paid through lives and lives, but I loved you then as I love you now." A Zbyszko hammer lock, and at long last their lips, parched with rhetoric, meet in a lingering kiss.

The note of implied finality, however, is only a ruse; if the fable is to come full circle, its characters must show the effect of their sojourn away from civilization. Just as the pair are being united by the preacher, a ship appears on the horizon. Lady Mary tries to dissuade her chieftain from signaling for help, but he knows the code and gallantly bows to it. "Babylon has fallen and Crichton must play the game," he announces, gently unyoking her arms and yoking the metaphors.

Transported back to England in an agile dissolve, master and servant promptly revert to type. Lady Mary agrees to wed Lord Brocklehurst, though she reveals her heartbreak to Lady Eileen, whose marriage to her chauffeur has spelled social obloquy. Crichton retaliates by proposing to Tweeny, and, in a penultimate scene, we see them between kisses, operating an Australian sheep farm. For the tag, or washup, De Mille chose a bittersweet dying fall. On the lawn of a vast country house, amid drifting petals, Lady Mary toys with her parasol and dreams of what might have been. The title reads, "You may break, you may shatter, the vase if you will, but the scent of the roses will hang around her still. Thus does the great sacrifice shed its fragrance over a lifetime." Enter a beflanneled Brocklehurst, who stands regarding her with doglike devotion. "I understand, my dear, why you postponed our marriage," he declares, manfully sweeping up the loose exposition. "You loved Crichton, the admirable Crichton. I'll be waiting for you at the judgment day." He raises her hand to his lips, Lady Mary's eyes under her picture hat fill with tears, and, to use a very apt technical term, we squeeze.

I suspect that a lot of people in my generation, the kind of romantics who blubber at the sight of a Maxfield Parrish print or a Jordan roadster, would not have withstood my sentimental excursion as gracefully as I did, and would have wound up fractured at the Jumble Shop, harmonizing "The Japanese Sandman." Matter of fact, I ran into a couple of these romantics at the Jumble Shop, strangely enough, right after seeing *Male and Female*. We got to talking, and darned if they hadn't seen it too as kids. Well, we had a bite of supper, took in the ice show at the Hotel New Yorker, and then, armed with plenty of ratchets, started back to the Museum about midnight so I could screen the picture for them. Luckily, their car hit a hydrant en route and I managed to slip away unnoticed. If I hadn't kept my wits about me, though, the whole day might have ended with much worse than eyestrain. As a middle-aged movie fan, I've learned one lesson: Lay off that nostalgia, cousin. It's lethal.

Roll on, Thou Deep
and Dark Scenario, Roll

ONE AUGUST morning during the third summer of the First World War, Manuel Da Costa, a Portuguese eel fisherman at Bullock's Cove, near Narragansett Bay, was calking a dory drawn up beside his shack when he witnessed a remarkable exploit. From around a nearby boathouse appeared a bumpkin named Piggy Westervelt, with a head indistinguishable from an Edam cheese, lugging a bicycle pump and a coil of rubber hose. Behind him, with dragging footsteps, because of the quantities of scrap iron stuffed into his boots, came another stripling, indistinguishable from the present writer at the age of twelve, encased in a diving helmet that was improvised from a metal lard pail. As Da Costa watched with fascinated attention, Piggy ceremoniously conducted me to the water's edge, helped me kneel, and started securing the hose to my casque.

"Can you breathe in there all right?" he called out anxiously. There was some basis for his concern, since, in the zeal of creation, we had neglected to supply a hinge for my visor, and between lack of oxygen and the reek of hot lard my eyes were beginning to extrude like muscat grapes. I signaled Piggy to hurry up and start pumping, but he became unaccountably angry. "How many hands do you think I got?" he bawled. "If you don't like the way I'm doing it, get somebody else!" Realizing my life hung on a lunatic's caprice, I adopted the only rational attitude, that of the sacrificial ox, and shallowed my breathing. Finally, just as the old mitral valve was about to close forever, a few puffs of fetid air straggled through the tube and I shakily prepared to submerge. My objective was an ancient weedy hull thirty feet offshore, where the infamous Edward Teach, popularly known as Blackbeard, was reputed to have foundered with a cargo of bullion and plate. Neither of us had the remotest idea what bullion and plate were, but they sounded eminently useful. I was also to keep a sharp lookout for ambergris, lumps of which were constantly being picked up by wide-awake boys and found to be worth forty thousand dollars. The prospects, viewed from whatever angle, were pretty rosy.

They began to dim the second I disappeared below the surface. By that time, the hose had sprung half a dozen leaks, and Piggy, in a frenzy of misdirected co-operation, had pumped my helmet full of water. Had I not been awash in the pail, I might have been able to squirm out of my boots, but as it was, I was firmly anchored in the ooze and a definite candidate for Davy Jones's locker when an unexpected savior turned up in the person of Manuel Da Costa. Quickly sculling overhead, he captured the hose with a boat hook, dragged me inboard, and pounded the water out of my lungs. The first sight I saw, as I lay gasping in the scuppers, was Manuel towering over me like the Colossus of Rhodes, arms compressed and lips akimbo. His salutation finished me forever as an undersea explorer. "Who the hell do you think you are?" he demanded, outraged. "Captain Nemo?"

That a Rhode Island fisherman should invoke anyone so

recherché as the hero of Jules Verne's submarine saga may seem extraordinary, but actually there was every justification for it. All through the preceding fortnight, a movie version of *Twenty Thousand Leagues Under the Sea* had been playing to packed houses at a local peepshow, engendering almost as much excitement as the Black Tom explosion. Everyone who saw it was dumfounded—less, I suspect, by its subaqueous marvels than by its hallucinatory plot and characters—but nobody besides Piggy and me, fortunately, was barmy enough to emulate it. In general, I experienced no untoward effects from my adventure. It did, however, prejudice me unreasonably against salt water, and for years I never mentioned the ocean floor save with a sneer.

Some weeks ago, rummaging through the film library of the Museum of Modern Art, I discovered among its goodies a print of the very production of *Twenty Thousand Leagues* that had mesmerized me in 1916, and, by ceaseless nagging, bedeviled the indulgent custodians into screening it for me. Within twenty minutes, I realized that I was watching one of the really great cinema nightmares, a *cauchemar* beside which *King Kong*, *The Tiger Man*, and *The Cat People* were as staid as so many quilting bees. True, it did not have the sublime irrelevance of *The Sex Maniac*, a masterpiece of Krafft-Ebing symbolism I saw in Los Angeles whose laboratory monkeyshines climaxed in a scene where two Picassoesque giantesses, armed with baseball bats, beat each other to pulp in a cellar. On the other hand, it more than equaled the all-time stowage record set by D. W. Griffith's *Intolerance*, managing to combine in one picture three unrelated plots—*Twenty Thousand Leagues*, *The Mysterious Island*, and *Five Weeks in a Balloon*—and a sanguinary tale of betrayal and murder in a native Indian state that must have fallen into the developing fluid by mistake. To make the whole thing even more perplexing, not one member of the cast was identified—much as if all the actors in the picture had been slain on its completion and all references to them expunged. I daresay that if Stuart Paton, its director, were functioning today, the votaries of the Surrealist film who sibilate around the Little Carnegie and the Fifth Avenue Playhouse would be weaving garlands for his hair. That man could make a cryptogram out of Mother Goose.

The premise of *Twenty Thousand Leagues*, in a series of quick nutshells, is that the Navy, dismayed by reports of a gigantic sea serpent preying on our merchant marine, dispatches an expedition to exterminate it. Included in the party are Professor Aronnax, a French scientist with luxuriant crepe hair and heavy eye make-up who looks like a phrenologist out of the funny papers; his daughter, a kittenish ingénue all corkscrew curls and maidenly simpers; and the latter's heartbeat, a broth of a boy identified as Ned Land, Prince of Harpooners. Their quarry proves, of course, to be the submarine *Nautilus*, commanded by the redoubtable Captain Nemo, which sinks their vessel and takes them prisoner. Nemo is Melville's Captain Ahab with French dressing, as bizarre a mariner as ever trod on a weevil. He has a profile like Garibaldi's, set off by a white goatee; wears a Santa Claus suit and a turban made out of a huck towel; and smokes a churchwarden pipe. Most submarine commanders, as a rule, busy themselves checking gauges and twiddling the periscope, but Nemo spends all his time smiting his forehead and vowing revenge, though on whom it is not made clear. The décor of the *Nautilus*, obviously inspired by a Turkish cozy corner, is pure early Matisse; Oriental rugs, hassocks, and mother-of-pearl taborets abound, and in one shot I thought I detected a parlor floor lamp with a fringed shade, which must have been a problem in dirty weather. In all justice, however, Paton's conception of a submarine interior was no more florid than Jules Verne's. Among the ship's accouterments, I find on consulting the great romancer, he lists a library containing twelve thousand volumes, a dining room with oak sideboards, and a thirty-foot drawing room full of Old Masters, tapestry, and sculpture.

Apparently, the front office figured that so straightforward a narrative would never be credible, because complications now really begin piling up. "About this time," a subtitle announces, "Lieutenant Bond and four Union Army scouts, frustrated in an attempt to destroy their balloon, are carried out to sea." A long and murky sequence full of lightning, falling sandbags, and disheveled character actors occupies the next few minutes, the upshot being that the cloud-borne quintet is stranded on a remote key called Mysterious Island. One of its more mysterious aspects is an unchaperoned young person in a leopardskin sarong, who dwells in the trees and mutters gibberish to herself. The castaways find this tropical Ophelia in a pit they have dug to ward off prowling beasts, and Lieutenant Bond, who obviously has been out of touch with women since he was weaned, loses his heart to her. To achieve greater obscurity, the foregoing is intercut with limitless footage of Captain Nemo and his hostages goggling at the wonders of the deep through a window in the side of the submarine. What they see is approximately what anybody might who has quaffed too much sacramental wine and is peering into a home aquarium, but, after all, tedium is a relative matter. When you come right down to it, a closeup of scup feeding around a coral arch is no more static than one of Robert Taylor.

At this juncture, a completely new element enters the plot to further befuddle it, in the form of one Charles Denver, "a retired ocean trader in a distant land." Twelve years earlier, a flashback reveals, Denver had got a skinful of lager and tried to ravish an Indian maharani called Princess Daaker. The lady had thereupon plunged a dagger into her thorax, and Denver, possibly finding the furniture too heavy, had stolen her eight-year-old daughter. We see him now in a mood of remorse approaching that of Macbeth, drunkenly clawing his collar and reviling the phantoms who plague him—one of them, by the way, a rather engaging Mephistopheles of the sort depicted in advertisements for quick-drying varnish. To avoid losing his mind, the trader boards his yacht and sets off for Mysterious Island, a very peculiar choice indeed, for if ever there was a convocation of loonies anywhere, it is there. Captain Nemo is fluthering around in the lagoon, wrestling with an inflated rubber octopus; Lieutenant Bond and the leopard girl (who, it presently emerges, is Princess Daaker's daughter, left there to die) are spooning on the cliffs; and, just to enliven things, one of Bond's scouts is planning to supplant him as leader and abduct the maiden.

Arriving at the island, Denver puts on a pippin of a costume, consisting of a deerstalker cap, a Prince Albert coat, and hip boots, and goes ashore to seek the girl he marooned. He has just vanished into the saw grass, declaiming away like Dion Boucicault, when the screen suddenly blacks out, or at least it did the day I saw the picture. I sprang up buoyantly, hoping that perhaps the film had caught fire and provided a solution for everybody's dilemma, but it had merely slipped off the sprocket. By the time it was readjusted, I, too, had slipped off, consumed a flagon or two, and was back in my chair waiting alertly for the payoff. I soon realized my blunder. I should have stayed in the rathskeller and had the projectionist phone it to me.

Denver becomes lost in the jungle very shortly, and when he fails to return to the yacht, two of the crew go in search of him. They meet Lieutenant Bond's scout, who has meanwhile made indecent overtures to the leopard girl and been declared a pariah by his fellows. The trio rescue Denver, but, for reasons that defy analysis, get plastered and plot to seize the yacht and sail away with the girl.

During all this katzenjammer, divers from the *Nautilus* have been reconnoitering around the craft to learn the identity of its owner, which presumably is emblazoned on its keel, inasmuch as one of them hastens to Nemo at top speed to announce with a flourish, "I have the honor to report that the yacht is owned by Charles Denver." The Captain forthwith stages a display of vindictive triumph that would have left Boris Thomashefsky, the great Yiddish tragedian, sick with envy; Denver, he apprises his companions, is the man against whom he has sworn undying vengeance. In the meantime (everything in *Twenty Thousand Leagues* happens in the meantime; the characters don't even sneeze consecutively), the villains kidnap the girl, are pursued to the yacht by Bond, and engage him in a fight to the death. At the psychological moment, a torpedo from the *Nautilus* blows up the whole shebang, extraneous characters are eliminated, and as the couple are hauled aboard the submarine, the big dramatic twist unfolds: Nemo is Prince Daaker and the girl his daughter. Any moviemaker with elementary decency would have recognized this as the saturation point and quit, but not the producer of *Twenty Thousand Leagues*. The picture bumbles on into a fantastically long-winded flashback of Nemo reviewing the whole Indian episode and relentlessly chewing the scenery to bits, and culminates with his demise and a strong suspicion in the onlooker that he has talked himself to death. His undersea burial, it must be admitted, has an authentic grisly charm. The efforts of the funeral party, clad in sober diving habit, to dig a grave in the ocean bed finally meet with defeat, and, pettishly tossing the coffin into a clump of sea anemones, they stagger off. It seemed to me a bit disrespectful not to blow "Taps" over the deceased, but I suppose nobody had a watertight bugle.

An hour after quitting the Museum, I was convalescing on a bench in Central Park when a brandy-nosed individual approached me with a remarkable tale of woe. He was, he declared, a by-blow of Prince Felix Youssoupoff, the assassin of Rasputin, and had been reared by Transylvanian gypsies. Successively a circus aerialist, a mosaic worker, a diamond cutter, and a gigolo, he had fought (or at least argued) with Wingate's Raiders, crossed Outer Mongolia on foot, spent two years in a Buddhist monastery, helped organize the Indonesian resistance, and become one of the financial titans of Lombard Street. A woman, he confided huskily, had been his undoing—a woman so illustrious that the mere mention of her name made Cabinets totter. His present financial embarrassment, however, was a purely temporary phase. Seversky had imported him to the States to design a new helicopter, and if I could advance him a dime to phone the designer that he had arrived, I would be amply reimbursed. As he vanished into oblivion cheerily jingling my two nickels, the old lady sharing my bench put down her knitting with a snort.

"Tommyrot!" she snapped. "Hunh, you must be a simpleton. That's the most preposterous balderdash I ever heard of."

"I *am* a simpleton, Madam," I returned with dignity, "but you don't know beans about balderdash. Let me tell you a movie I just saw." No sooner had I started to recapitulate it than her face turned ashen, and without a word of explanation she bolted into the shrubbery. An old screwbox, obviously. Oh, well, you can't account for anything nowadays. Some of the stuff that goes on, it's right out of a novel by Jules Verne.

Vintage Swine

SOME Hollywood flack, in a burst of inspiration, dubbed him the Man You Love to Hate. He was a short man, almost squat, with a vulpine smirk that told you, the moment his image flashed upon the screen, that no wife or bank roll must be left unguarded. The clean-shaven bullethead, the glittering monocle, and the ramrod back (kept rigid by a corset, it was whispered) were as familiar and as dear to the moviegoing public as the Pickford curls or Eugene O'Brien's pompadour. No matter what the background of the picture was—an English drawing room, a compartment on the Orient Express, the legation quarter of Peiping—he always wore tight-fitting military tunics, flaunted an ivory cigarette holder, and kissed ladies' hands profusely, betraying them in the next breath with utter impartiality. For sheer menace, he made even topnotch vipers like Lew Cody, Ivan Lebedeff, and Rockliffe Fellowes seem rank stumblebums by comparison. He was the ace of cads, a man without a single redeeming feature, the embodiment of Prussian Junkerism, and the greatest heavy of the silent film, and his name, of course, was Erich von Stroheim.

I first saw him in a tempestuous drama, presented by Carl La-emmle in 1919, called *Blind Husbands*, which von Stroheim, with cyclonic energy, had adapted into a photoplay, and directed, from *The Pinnacle*, a novel he had also written. Actually, I must have seen him three years earlier as the Second Pharisee in the Judean movement of *Intolerance*, wearing a fright wig and a gaudy toga and heckling the Nazarene, but there was so much Biblical flapdoodle flying around that I was too confused to peg him.

The picture that definitely canonized von Stroheim for me, though, was *Foolish Wives*, a gripping exposé of the swindlers who were popularly supposed to prey on rich Americans in Monte Carlo. In this 1922 chef-d'oeuvre, he impersonated a spurious Russian noble named Ladislaw Sergius Von Karamzin, as ornery a skunk as ever flicked a riding crop against a boot. Everything about him seemed to me touched with enchantment: his stiff-necked swagger, his cynical contempt for the women he misused, and, above all, his dandyism—the monogrammed cigarettes, the dressing gowns with silk lapels, the musk he sprayed himself with to heighten his allure. For six months afterward, I exhibited a maddening tendency to click my heels and murmur "*Bitte?*" along with a twitch as though a monocle were screwed into my eye. The mannerisms finally abated, but not until the Dean of Brown University had taken me aside and confided that if I wanted to transfer to Heidelberg, the faculty would not stand in my way.

Not long ago, the Museum of Modern Art graciously permitted me to run its copy of *Foolish Wives*, on condition that if I became overstimulated or mushy, I would not pick the veneer off the chairs or kiss the projectionist. Such fears, it presently turned out, were baseless. The showing roused me to neither vandalism nor affection; in fact, it begot such lassitude that I had to be given artificial respiration and sent home in a wheelbarrow. Ordinarily, I would incline to put the blame on my faulty metabolism, but this time I knew what the trouble was. A certain satanic *Schweinhund* hadn't blitzed me as he used to thirty years ago.

Foolish Wives upsets precedent by first investigating the seamy side of Monte Carlo instead of its glamour. We fade in on a milieu brimful of plot—the tenebrous hovel of an aged counterfeiter named Ventucci. A visit from his principal client, Count Karamzin, establishes that the latter is using Ventucci's green goods to support an opulent villa as a front for his stratagems. During their colloquy, the Count's jaded appetite is whetted by his host's nineteen-year-old daughter, a poor daft creature fondling a rag doll. The old man stiffens. "She is my only treasure," he snaps at von Stroheim, unsheathing a stiletto. "If anyone should harm her . . ." Leaving this promissory note to be honored at whatever point von Stroheim has run his gamut, the action shifts to an exclusive hotel near the casino. Here we meet an overripe young matron with a face like a matzoth pancake, all bee-stung lips and mascara, the wife of an American millionaire called (*sic*) Howard Hughes, and played by a sluggish *Rheinmaedchen* identified in the cast of characters only as Miss Dupont. Von Stroheim ogles the lady, who seems complaisant, gets himself presented to her, and, baiting his hook with a sermon about the pitfalls of Monte Carlo, offers to introduce her to his cousins the Princesses Olga and Vera Petchnikoff. He furthermore assures her, brazenly squinting down her bodice, that they—and, of course, he—would be enraptured to act as her social sponsors. Mrs. Hughes, understandably, is *bouleversée*, and, consenting to accompany him to a water carnival several nights thence, lumbers away to loosen her stays and recover her wits. Whether she has any of either is debatable; both her figure and her deportment are so flabby that one cannot work up much moral indignation against von Stroheim. The man is earning a very hard dollar.

Disclosed next is the Villa Amorosa, the seaside lair of the Count and his confederates, Princess Olga (Maude George) and Princess Vera (Mae Busch). For my money, Mae Busch never possessed the spidery, ghoulish fascination of that consummate she-devil Jetta Goudal, but she ranked high as a delineator of adventuresses and Eurasian spies. At any rate, the two lady trick-sters, far from being von Stroheim's cousins, live in what appears to be a languid state of concubinage, switching about in negligees and exchanging feline gibes. Over breakfast, the three agree on the *modus operandi* standard among movie blackmailers, whereby the Princesses are to divert Mr. Hughes while von Stroheim com-promises his wife. Ventucci, meanwhile, bustles into focus in the crisp, matter-of-fact fashion of a milkman, trailed by his daughter and bringing a satchel of fresh queer just off the press. He gives off ominous rumblings when the Count behaves familiarly with the girl, but nothing more consequential than glowering results. The same is true of the water carnival that evening. Mr. Hughes, a silver-haired, phlegmatic wowser, whose civilian name escaped me in the credits, betrays mild pique at the sight of his wife pad-dling around the studio tank and pelting von Stroheim with artifi-cial roses but, after a few heavy sarcasms, relapses into coma. Had the tempo not quickened in the ensuing scene, the picture might have ended right there for me. What with the whir of the projector and the weight of my eyelids, it took every bit of buckram I had, plus frequent pulls at a Benzedrine inhaler, to keep from sliding into the abyss.

Whittled down to essentials, the purport of the scene is that the Count takes Mrs. Hughes on an afternoon excursion, pretends to get lost in a thunderstorm, and steers her to a sinister house of assignation run by a crone called Mother Gervaise. The sole function of this unsavory character, as far as I could tell, was to persuade the young matron to doff her wet shimmy, so that von Stroheim, who has made a great show of turning his back, can stealthily appraise her in a pocket mirror—as neat a sample of voyeurism, I may add, as any ever reported by Wilhelm Stekel. After endless chin music calculated to allay her trepidation, von Stroheim has just maneuvered his sweetmeat into the horizontal when a wild-eyed anchorite reels in, ululating for shelter. Who this holy man is the picture never explains, but his scowls put a quietus on the high jinks, and Mrs. Hughes regains her hotel next morning shopworn but chaste. Inexplicably enough, the Count does not use the incident to shake down her husband—indeed, he has Princess Vera affirm that Mrs. Hughes spent the night with her—and the whole affair mystifyingly trails off with nobody the wiser, least of all the audience.

Up to now, the element of gambling has been so ruthlessly slighted in the story that the locale might as well have been a Scottish tabernacle or the annual dance festival at Jacob's Pillow. Suddenly, however, Lady Luck rears her head beside that of Sex. In addition to his other *chinoiserie*, von Stroheim has been shacking up with a bedraggled maiden named Malishka, a servant at the villa, whom he has glibly promised to wed as soon as the Bolsheviki are deposed. To still her importunities, the Count cooks up a pitiable tale of insolvency and borrows her life savings, which he loses at roulette. Mrs. Hughes, who is also having a flutter at the wheel, observes his despair and lends him her pile of counters—a gesture that abruptly changes his luck. Strong though the temptation is to pocket his winnings, he craftily relinquishes them to his benefactress, and then, a few hours later, lures her to the Villa Amorosa with a plea that his life and honor are at stake. The rendezvous takes place in a tower room. Outside the door, Malishka crouches in a fever of jealousy, and this time generates sparks in a quite literal sense. Infuriated by her lover's endearments to Mrs. Hughes prior to easing her of ninety thousand francs, the maid locks the pair in and sets fire to the stairs. They take refuge on an exterior balcony, from which they shout appeals for help, but the other guests at the villa are absorbed in being fleeced at baccarat by the Princesses and fail to respond. Hughes, meanwhile, has become increasingly worried about his wife's absence, pantomiming his solicitude by sitting on the edge of his bed and thoughtfully scratching his chin. Eventually, the Monte Carlo Fire Department, which has been snoozing under the bull-dog edition of *Le Petit Monégasque*, bestirs itself, and, dashing to the scene, spreads a net under the balcony. Von Stroheim gallantly knees his companion aside and jumps first. Mrs. Hughes follows, almost hurtling through the roof of the limousine in which her husband has just driven up. Apart from the indignity of the *pompiers'* catching a glimpse of her bloomers, though, she sustains no perceptible damage, and the episode peters out, like all those preceding it, with Morpheus, the patron saint of the scenario, drowsily sharpening his quill for the next sequence.

Low as were the price of film and the salaries of actors in 1922, Mr. Laemmle and his aides must nevertheless have decided at this point in *Foolish Wives* that the consumer's patience was finite, and ordered the curtain down. The last reel, therefore, begins with Hughes's discovery, in his wife's corsage (while hunting for his pipe or a pair of shoe trees, I got the impression), of the note by which the Count had enticed her to his villa. He seeks out von Stroheim, knocks him down, and exposes his activities to the police. The Princesses are apprehended on the verge of flight, and unmasked as a couple of actresses named Maude George and Mae Busch, and now all that early scaffolding about Ventucci and his fey daughter comes in handy. Von Stroheim, in a stormy Dostoevskian finish, sneaks back to the coiner's hovel, ravishes the girl, is disemboweled by her father, and winds up being stuffed into a cistern. The concluding shot shows the Hugheses reunited—if two pieces of strudel can be said to be en rapport—lying in bed and reading, from a volume entitled *Foolish Wives*, the passage "And thus it happened that disillusionment came finally to a foolish wife who found in her husband that nobility she had sought for in—a counterfeit."

The vehicle creaks and possibly should have been left to molder in the carriage loft, yet it confirmed one opinion I had treasured for three decades. Whatever von Stroheim's shortcomings were as an artist, he was consistent. When he set out to limn a louse, he put his back into it. He never palliated his villainy, never helped old ladies across the street to show that he was a sweet kid *au fond* or prated about his Oedipus complex like the Percy boys who portray heavies today. I remember Grover Jones, a scenarist of long experience, once coaching me in Hollywood in the proper method of characterizing the menace in a horse opera. "The minute he pulls in on the Overland Stage," expounded Jones, "he should dismount and kick the nearest dog." Von Stroheim not only kicked the dog; he kicked the owner and the S.P.C.A. for good measure.

With the things he has on his conscience, I don't suppose the man ever slept a wink. But after all, nobody needs a whole lot of sleep to keep going. You can always drop off for a jiffy—especially if there's a projector and a can of old film around.

The Wickedest Woman in Larchmont

IF YOU were born anywhere near the beginning of the century and had access at any time during the winter of 1914–15 to thirty-five cents in cash, the chances are that after a legitimate deduction for nonpareils you blew in the balance on a movie called *A Fool There Was*. What gave the picture significance, assuming that it had any, was neither its story, which was paltry, nor its acting, which was aboriginal, but a pyrogenic half pint by the name of Theda Bara, who immortalized the vamp just as Little Egypt, at the World's Fair in 1893, had the hoochie-coochie. My own discovery of Miss Bara dates back to the sixth grade at grammar school and was due to a boy named Raymond Bugbee, a detestable bully who sat at the desk behind mine. Bugbee was a fiend incarnate, a hulking evil-faced youth related on both sides of his family to Torquemada and dedicated to making my life insupportable. He had perfected a technique of catapulting BB shot through his teeth with such force that some of them are still imbedded in my poll, causing a sensation like *tic douloureux* when it rains. Day after day, under threat of the most ghastly reprisals if I squealed, I was pinched, gouged, and nicked with paper clips, spitballs, and rubber bands. Too wispy to stand up to my oppressor, I took refuge in a subdued blubbering, which soon abraded the teacher's nerves and earned me the reputation of being refractory. One day, Bugbee finally overreached himself. Attaching a steel pen point to the welt of his shoe, he jabbed it upward into my posterior. I rose into the air caterwauling and, in the attendant ruckus, was condemned to stay after school and clap erasers. Late that afternoon, as I was numbly toiling away in a cloud of chalk dust, I accidentally got my first intimation of Miss Bara from a couple of teachers excitedly discussing her.

"If you rearrange the letters in her name, they spell 'Arab Death,'" one of them was saying, with a delicious shudder. "I've never seen an actress kiss the way she does. She just sort of glues herself onto a man and drains the strength out of him."

"I know—isn't it revolting?" sighed the other rapturously. "Let's go see her again tonight!" Needless to add, I was in the theater before either of them, and my reaction was no less fervent. For a full month afterward, I gave myself up to fantasies in which I lay with my head pillowed in the seductress's lap, intoxicated by coal-black eyes smoldering with belladonna. At her bidding, I eschewed family, social position, my brilliant career—a rather hazy combination of African explorer and private sleuth—to follow her to the ends of the earth. I saw myself, oblivious of everything but the nectar of her lips, being cashiered for cheating at cards (I was also a major in the Horse Dragoons), descending to drugs, and ultimately winding up as a beachcomber in the South Seas, with a saintly, ascetic face like H. B. Warner's. Between Bugbee's persecutions that winter and the moral quicksands I floundered into as a result of *A Fool There Was*, it's a wonder I ever lived through to Arbor Day.

A week or so ago, seeking to ascertain whether my inflammability to Miss Bara had lessened over the years, I had a retrospective look at her early triumph. Unfortunately, I could not duplicate the original conditions under which I had seen her, since the Museum of Modern Art projection room is roach-free and lacks those powerful candy-vending machines on the chairs that kicked like a Colt .45. Nonetheless, I managed to glean a fairly comprehensive idea of what used to accelerate the juices in 1915, and anyone who'd like a taste is welcome to step up to the tureen and skim off a cupful.

Produced by William Fox and based on the play by Porter Emerson Browne, *A Fool There Was* maunders through a good sixth of its footage establishing a whole spiral nebula of minor characters before it centers down on its two luminaries, the Vampire and the Fool. As succinctly as I can put it, the supporting players are the latter's wife Kate, an ambulatory laundry bag played by Mabel Frenyear; their daughter, an implacably arch young hoyden of nine, unidentified; Kate's sister (May Allison); her beau, a corpulent slob, also anonymous; and a headlong butler seemingly afflicted with locomotor ataxia. All these inhabit a depressing chalet in Larchmont, where, as far as I could discover, they do nothing but shake hands effusively. A tremendous amount of handshaking, by the way, distinguished the flicks in their infancy; no director worth his whipcord breeches would have dreamed of beginning a plot before everybody had exchanged greetings like a French wedding party entering a café. In any case, the orgy of salutation has just begun to die down when John Schuyler, the Fool, arrives by yacht to join his kin, and the handshaking starts all over again. Schuyler (Edward José), a florid, beefy lawyer in a high Belmont collar, is hardly what you would envision as passion's plaything, but I imagine it took stamina to be a leading man for Theda Bara—someone she could get her teeth into, so to speak. We now ricochet to the Vampire and her current victim, Parmalee (Victor Benoit), strolling on a grassy sward nearby. The siren, in billowing draperies and a period hat, carries almost as much sail as the *Golden Hind*, making it a bit difficult to assess her charms; however, they seem to have unmanned the young ne'er-do-well with her to the point where he is unable to light the Zira he is fumbling with. Their affair, it appears, has burned itself out, and Parmalee, wallowing in self-pity, is being given the frappé. Midway through his reproaches, a chauffeur-driven Simplex, sparkling with brass, pulls alongside, Miss Bara shoves him impatiently into it, and the pair whisk off screen. These turgid formalities completed, the picture settles down to business, and high time. In another moment, I myself would have been shaking hands and manumitting the projectionist to the ball game I was keeping him from.

In a telegram from the President (Woodrow Wilson presumably chose his envoys in an extremely haphazard manner), Schuyler is ordered to England on some delicate mission, such as fixing the impost on crumpets, and makes ready to leave. He expects to be accompanied by Kate and his daughter, but just prior to sailing, his sister-in-law clumsily falls out of the tonneau of her speedster, and Kate remains behind to nurse her. The Vampire reads of Schuyler's appointment, and decides to cross on the same vessel and enmesh him in her toils. As she enters the pier, an aged derelict accosts her, observing mournfully, "See what you have made of me—and still you prosper, you hellcat." Meanwhile, Par-

malee, learning of her desertion from a Japanese servant whose
eyelids are taped back with two pieces of court plaster, smashes
all the bric-a-brac and ferns in their love nest, tears down the portieres, and hastens to intercept her. The derelict waylays him at
the gangplank. "I might have known you'd follow her, Parmalee,"
he croaks. "Our predecessor, Van Diemen, rots in prison for
her." The plea to desist from his folly falls on deaf ears; Parmalee
sequesters his Circe on the promenade deck and, clapping a pistol
to his temple, declares his intention of destroying himself if she
abandons him. She smilingly flicks it aside with a rose and a line
of dialogue that is unquestionably one of the most hallowed in
dramaturgy: "Kiss me, my fool." Willful boy that he is, however,
Parmalee must have his own way and shoots himself dead. The
gesture, sad to say, is wasted, exciting only desultory interest. The
body is hustled off the ship, a steward briskly mops up the deck,
and by the time the *Gigantic* has cleared Sandy Hook, Theda and
her new conquest are making googly eyes and preparing to frac-
ture the Seventh Commandment by sending their laundry to the
same *blanchisseuse* in Paris.

A time lapse of two months, and in a hideaway on the Italian
Riviera choked with rubber plants and jardinieres, the lovers play
amorous tag like Dido and Aeneas, and nibble languidly on each
other's ears. Although everything seems to be leeches and cream,
a distinct undercurrent of tension is discernible between them;
Schuyler dreams betimes of Suburbia, his dusky cook who used
to make such good flapjacks, and when Theda jealously tears up
a letter from his wife, acrimony ensues. Soon after, while regis-
tering at a hotel, Schuyler is recognized by acquaintances, who,
much to his anguish, recoil as from an adder. Back in Westchester, Kate has learned of his peccadilloes through a gossip sheet.

She confronts Schuyler's law partner and, with typical feminine chauvinism, lambastes the innocent fellow: "You men shield each other's sins, but if the woman were at fault, how quick you'd be to condemn her!" Mrs. Schuyler's behavior, in fact, does little to ingratiate her. Not content with barging into a busy law office and disrupting its routine, she then runs home and poisons a child's mind against its father. "Mama," inquires her daughter, looking up from one of Schuyler's letters, "is a cross a sign for love?" "Yes," Kate retorts spitefully, "and love often means a cross." The fair sex (God bless them) can be really extraordinary at times.

In our next glimpse of the lotus-eaters, in London, Schuyler has already begun paying the piper; his eyes are berimmed with kohl, his step is palsied, and his hair is covered with flour. Theda, contrariwise, is thriving like the green bay tree, still tearing up his correspondence and wrestling him into embraces that char the woodwork. Their idyl is abruptly cut short by a waspish cable from the Secretary of State, which reads, in a code easily decipherable to the audience, "ON ACCOUNT OF YOUR DISGRACEFUL CONDUCT, YOU ARE HEREBY DISMISSED." Remorse and *Heimweh*, those twin powerful antibiotics, temporarily dispel the kissing bug that has laid Schuyler low. He returns to the States determined to rid himself of his incubus, but she clings and forces him to install her in a Fifth Avenue mansion. Humiliations multiply as she insists on attending the opera with him in a blaze of aigrettes, and there is an affecting scene when their phaeton is overtaken by his wife's auto near the Public Library and his daughter entreats him, "Papa, dear, I want you." But the call of the wild is too potent, and despite pressure from in-laws and colleagues alike, Schuyler sinks deeper into debauchery. Kate, meanwhile, is keening away amid a houseful of relatives, all of them shaking hands as dement-

edly as ever and proffering unsound advice. There is such a hol-
lering and a rending of garments and a tohubohu in the joint that
you can't really blame Schuyler for staying away. When a man has
worn himself down to the rubber struggling in a vampire's toils,
he wants to come home to a place where he can read his paper in
peace, not a loony bin.

Six months of revelry and an overzealous make-up man have
left their stamp on the Fool when we again see him; the poor chap
is shipping water fast. He reels around the mansion squirting
seltzer at the help and boxing with double-exposure phantoms,
and Theda, whose interest in her admirers wanes at the drop of a
security, is already stalking a new meatball. Apprised of the situation, Kate goes to her husband bearing an olive branch, but their
reunion is thwarted by his mistress, who unexpectedly checks
in and kisses him back into submission. The action now grows
staccato; Schuyler stages a monumental jamboree, at which his
guests drink carboys of champagne and dance the bunny hug very
fast, and then, overcome by delirium tremens, he violently expels
them into the night. Kate, in the meantime, has decided to take his
daughter to him as a last appeal. Preceded by her sister's beau (the
Slob), the pair arrive at the mansion to find Schuyler in parlous
shape. The child throws herself on him—a dubious service to anyone suffering from the horrors—and the adults beseech the wastrel to come home and, one infers, be committed to a nice, quiet
milieu where his expenditures can be regulated. His dilemma is
resolved by the reappearance of Theda; Schuyler grovels before
her, eradicating any doubt as to his fealty, and the folks exit
checkmated. The last few seconds of the picture, in a somber key
unmatched outside the tragedies of D'Annunzio, depict the Fool,
obsessed by a montage of his sins, squirming on his belly through

an openwork balustrade and collapsing in a vestibule. "So some of him lived," comments a final sepulchral title, "but the soul of him died." And over what remains, there appears a grinning presentment of Miss Bara, impenitent and sleek in black velvet and pearls, strewing rose petals as we fade out.

For all its bathos and musty histrionics, *A Fool There Was*, I am convinced, still retains some mysterious moral sachet, if the experience I had after seeing it is at all indicative. As I was quietly recuperating in a West Side snug over a thimble of sherry and the poems of St. John Perse, a young woman who was manifestly no better than she should be slid into the banquette adjoining mine. So absorbed was I in the poet's meter that it was almost two minutes before I detected her wanton gaze straying toward me in unmistakable invitation. I removed my spectacles and carefully placed them in their shagreen case. "Mademoiselle," I said, "the flirtation you propose, while ostensibly harmless, could develop unless checked into a dangerous liaison. I am a full-blooded man, and one who does not do things by halves. Were I to set foot on the primrose path, scenes of carnival and license to shame Petronius might well ensue. No, my dear young lady," I said, draining my glass and rising, "succulent morsel though you are, I have no desire to end my days like John Schuyler, crawling through balustrades and being sprinkled with blooms." As luck would have it, her escort, whose existence I had somehow neglected to allow for, materialized behind me at this juncture and, pinioning me, questioned my motives. I gave him a brief résumé of *A Fool There Was* to amplify my position, but he acted as though I had invented the whole thing. Maybe I have. Still, who could have made up Theda Bara?

I'm Sorry I Made Me Cry

THE CONSULTING room I sat in that dun December afternoon in 1920 was a perfect setting for a senior Rhode Island eye specialist, and Dr. Adrian Budlong was perfectly cast in the role of the specialist. A septuagenarian with a sunken, emaciated face, and as angular as a praying mantis, Dr. Budlong bore a chilling resemblance to the mummified Rameses II, and it would not have surprised me to learn that he kept his entrails in an alabaster canopic jar under his desk. The room itself was rather like a crypt, dark and redolent of musty bindings and iodoform; behind the Doctor's head, in the shadows, a bust of Galen just large enough for a raven to perch on scowled down at me balefully. For forty-five minutes, Dr. Budlong, in an effort to discover why my eyelids were swollen like Smyrna figs, had submitted me to every test known to ophthalmology. He had checked my vision with all manner of graduated charts and images, made me swivel my eyeballs until they bellied from their sockets, peered endlessly into my irises with sinister flashlights. The examination, clearly, had been fruitless, for he was now bombarding me with questions that struck me as irrelevant, if not fatuous. Had

I eaten any toadstools recently, been stung by any wasps or hornets? Had I wittingly stepped on a rattlesnake or serpent of any description?

"I—I swim under water a lot at the Y.M.C.A.," I faltered. "Maybe the disinfectant—"

"Chlorine never hurt anybody," he snapped. "Clears the brain." With a palsied clawlike hand, he plucked the optical mirror from his death's-head and dropped it on the blotter. "Humph—no reason a boy of your age should suddenly start looking like a bullfrog. Have you been under any mental strain lately? What kind of stuff d'ye read?"

"Er—mostly history," I said evasively. "Balzac's *Droll Stories*, the *Decameron*, Brantôme's *Lives of Fair and Gallant Ladies*—"

"Nothing there that would affect the lids especially," he said, with what I considered unnecessary coarseness. "Now let's stop paltering around, young man. What have you been crying about?" Somewhere deep in my consciousness, a louver flew open and I saw the façade of the Providence Opera House, the temple where every moviegoer in town had been snuffling uncontrollably over D. W. Griffith's great tear-jerker *Way Down East*. Choking back a sob, I confessed shamefacedly that I had seen the picture three times. Dr. Budlong regarded me for a full twenty minutes in silence, patently undecided whether to have me certified or bastinadoed. Then, making no effort to conceal his spleen, he prescribed cold poultices and a moratorium on cinematic pathos, and flung me out. By an evil circumstance, the trolley car that bore me homeward passed the Opera House. Hours later, streaked with tears, and blubbering from my fourth exposure to the masterpiece, I informed my folks that Budlong had pronounced me a victim of winter hay fever. The diagnosis aroused no visible furor. By then the family was impervious to shock.

Not long ago, examining the network of laughter lines around my eyes in the mirror, it occurred to me that I was in peril of becoming a slippered popinjay. Life since forty had been so rollicking and mirthful that I had allowed my sentimental, nobler instincts to retrogress; what I needed, and pronto, was a profound emotional *nettoyage*. Accordingly, I downed twenty pages of Thomas Merton, the spiritual equivalent of sulphur and molasses, listened to Jan Peerce's superbly emetic recording of "What Is a Boy?" and topped it off with a matinée of *Way Down East* at the Museum of Modern Art. I can get around the house passably by holding on to the furniture, but I still feel a mite queasy.

The leitmotiv of *Way Down East*, like that of so many early film melodramas, was innocence betrayed, virtue—doggedly sullied through ten reels—rising triumphant and kneeing its traducer in the groin. The sweet resignation with which Lillian Gish, the heroine, underwent every vicissitude of fortune from bastardy to frostbite, and the lacquered, mandarin composure of Richard Barthelmess in the face of ostracism and blizzard, have rarely been surpassed on celluloid. It was, however, Lowell Sherman, that peerless actor, who, in his delineation of the villain, copped the honors. Exquisitely groomed, a trifle flaccid, the epitome of the jaded roué, he moved catlike through the action, stalking his prey, his face a mask of smiling insincerity that occasionally let slip a barbered sneer. When he tapped a cigarette deliberately on his silver case and cast a cool, speculative glance into a woman's bodice, you knew she would never survive the rabbit test. Sidney

Blackmer, Henry Daniell, Robert Morley—there have been many able varmints since, but none quite as silky or loathsome as Lowell Sherman. They had to spray him with fungicide between takes to keep the mushrooms from forming on him.

Way Down East, billed in its opening title as "a simple story for plain people" (the adjectives would seem to be interchangeable), starts off with a windy hundred-and-twenty-two-word essay containing far less juice than pulp and seeds. Its general content is that while polygamy is on the wane, monogamy is not yet worldwide—an assertion calculated to lacerate nobody's feelings, whether Bedouin or Baptist. The locale of the drama, continues the preamble, is "in the story world of make-believe; characters nowhere, yet everywhere." Having slaked the passion for universality that constantly assailed him, Griffith yielded the stage to his puppets. Anna Moore (Miss Gish) and her widowed mother, destitute in a New England village, decide to put the sleeve on the Tremonts, their rich Boston relatives. Clad in gingham and a black wide-awake straw, Anna sets off for their mansion, bumbling into a stylish musicale they are giving and discomfiting her snobbish female cousins. In order to make character with a rich, eccentric aunt, however, the Tremonts swallow their resentment and take Anna in. Simultaneously, the girl has a fleeting encounter with her seducer-to-be, dashing Lennox Sanderson (Lowell Sherman), who smirks into her cleavage and earmarks her for future spoliation. We now whisk to the countervailing influence in Anna's life, David Bartlett (Richard Barthelmess), as he scratches a pigeon's neck on his father's farm, adjacent to Sanderson's country estate. "Though of plain stock," the subtitle explains, "he has been tutored by poets and vision wide as the world." He has also had access, it might be noted, to a remarkable pomade, which keeps his hair snugly plastered to his scalp no matter how turbulent the action becomes. The secret of Barthelmess's hair has never ceased to fascinate me. In every picture I recall him in, from *Broken Blossoms* and *Tol'able David* to *The Idol Dancer* and *The Love Flower*, nothing ever disturbed that sleek coiffure. Cockney bruisers beat the daylights out of Barthelmess, bullying mates kicked him down hatchways and flailed him with marlinspikes, and Papuans boiled him in kettles, but he always looked as though he had just emerged from the Dawn Patrol Barbershop. Of course, there is no external evidence that his hair was real; it may merely have been Duco, sprayed on him between takes, like Sherman's fungicide, but how they ever prevented it from cracking is beyond me.

Anna's downfall, the next item on the agenda, is one of the most precipitous and brutal since the sack of Constantinople by the Turks. Sanderson spies her at a society rout, almost unbearably ethereal in soft focus and a cloud of tulle, and, closing in, murmurs thickly, "In your beauty lives again Elaine, the Lily Maid, love-dreaming at Astolat." Enchanted by this verbal zircon, Anna dimples from head to toe and implores, "Tell me more." He obliges, with such notable effect that she ultimately agrees to a secret marriage ceremony, unaware that the parson is bogus and the witnesses fixed. From then on, the poor creature is fed through the dramatic wringer with relentless ferocity. After her return home, she finds she is gravid, appeals to Sanderson—who, meanwhile, has gone on to other amorous diversions—and discovers that she has been euchred. Sanderson callously deserts her, on the pretext that he will be disinherited if their liaison comes to light, and Anna's mother, with typical maternal spitefulness, dies off just when she is most needed. The baby languishes from birth; when it succumbs, giving Anna endless golden opportunities for

histrionics, she is expelled from her lodgings by a righteous landlady, and the first portion of her Gethsemane concludes. The least
sophisticated movie fan senses, though, that his tear ducts are
being permitted only the briefest respite. Better than any director
before or since, Griffith understood the use of the bean ball, and
he now prepares to pitch it square at his leading lady and reduce
everyone to jelly.

Drawn by the peculiar magnetism that polarizes movie characters, Anna wanders to the Bartlett farm, meets David, and so
generally excites pity that Squire Bartlett, his gruff, bigoted father,
gives her a minor post agitating a churn. The farm hums with all
sorts of romantic activity. There is, for instance, a visiting niece
named Kate who is alternately being courted by Hi Holler, the
hired man, and the Professor, an absent-minded pedagogue with
a butterfly net. Gusty bucolic comedy ensues when the former,
daubing his shoes and hair with axle grease to enhance his charm,
is struck on the head by a new-laid egg and backs into a pitchfork.
Also on hand to provoke chuckles is a rustic twosome made up of
Martha Perkins, the village gossip, and her perennial admirer, a
hayseed in a linen duster who quaffs Long Life Bitters. The story
meanders sluggishly along for a spell, washing up tender symbols
like cooing buds and bursting doves to blueprint David's bias for
Anna, and then Lennox Sanderson pops in again, this time mous-
ing around after Kate. He berates Anna for remaining in his bai-
liwick and, in truly heartless fashion, orders her to clear off. As
she is about to, though, David shyly confesses his *béguin* for her
(and nobody could confess a *béguin* more shyly than Barthelmess,
without moving so much as a muscle in his face). At length, sorely
troubled, she decides to stay—a difficult decision and similar to

one that I myself, by a coincidence, was having to make. Confidentially, it was touch and go.

Except for love's gradual ripening, the next thousand feet of the film are as devoid of incident as a Fitzpatrick travel talk on Costa Rica, Land of the Coffee Bean. There is a plethora of fields choked with daisies, misty-eyed colloquies, and orotund subtitles like "One heart for one heart, one soul for one soul, one love, even through eternity. At last the great overwhelming love, only to be halted by the stark ghost of her past." With the onset of winter, the plot registers a sudden galvanic twitch. Just as Anna is stalemated between David's proposal, which she cannot bring herself to accept, and Sanderson's renewed persecutions, her onetime landlady happens into the village, recognizes her, and recounts her shame to the sewing circle. Martha Perkins, of course, instantly hurries to the Squire to apprise him that he is harboring a Jezebel, and the fat is in the fire. Anna is excoriated in front of the entire household and driven forth despite David's protestations, but not before she castigates Sanderson as her betrayer. A blizzard, which has been picking its teeth in the wings, now comes in on cue, and enfolding the outcast, whirls her toward the icebound river. David, who meanwhile has been locked in mortal combat with Sanderson (without having his hair mussed, naturally), flattens his adversary and runs to intercept Anna; the ice goes out, she is swept to the brink of the falls, and her lover, exhibiting the nimblest footwork since Packy McFarland, saves her from annihilation. The rest of the spool portrays Sanderson, surprisingly natty after his drubbing, offering his dupe legitimate wedlock and sighing with relief when she disdains him, and a multiple marriage in which Anna and David, Kate and the Professor, and Martha and her apple-knocker are united. So ends the morality, with no hard feelings except in the gluteus, and with that unique sense of degradation that attends a trip to the movies during daylight.

As it happens, the only known antidote for the foregoing is a double banana split with oodles of fudge sauce, and immediately on quitting *Way Down East* I sought one out at a neighboring drugstore. As I was burrowing into it like a snowplow, I became conscious of the soda jerker's intent scrutiny. "Say, din I use to see you around the old Opera House in Providence?" he inquired narrowly. "I took tickets there when I was a kid." Judging from the man's decrepitude, I would have had to dandle Bronson Alcott on my knee to be his contemporary, but I waived the point and held still for a spate of theatrical reminiscence. At last, as a sort of tourniquet, I mentioned *Way Down East* and suggested he might enjoy seeing it again. He drew himself up, offended. "Listen, wise guy," he retorted. "I may handle slop for a living, but I don't have to look at it." I slunk out with flaming cheeks, made even pinker by the cashier's recalling me to settle the check. Altogether, it was a shattering afternoon. The next time my nobler nature gets the upper hand, I aim for the nearest Turkish bath.

By the Waters of Razz-Ma-Tazz

TOWARD the end of 1920, or just about the time the fencing foils on my bedroom wall were yielding to sepia portraits of Blanche Sweet and Carol Dempster, I became briefly enamored of a Rhode Island schoolmate named, if memory serves, Celia Cahoon. Together with a dozen other unemployables that semester, Miss Cahoon and I were retracing Xenophon's footsteps to the sea, and as we toiled our daily twenty parasangs over the stony Mesopotamian plain, leaving a wake of dead and dying gerunds, I felt myself involuntarily succumbing to her spell. Though hardly the comeliest girl in the class, Celia possessed a figure so voluptuous that it addled every male within a radius of fifty feet. Whenever she was called on to recite, chairs began to scrape, pencils rolled off the desks, people upset ink on their pants, and the quickened exhalations formed a steam that fogged the windows. In her senior year at Classical High, Celia undoubtedly came in for more accidental jostling in corridor and lunchroom than anyone prior to Sophia Loren.

It was, therefore, with as much exultation as though I had been singled out of the ranks by Catherine of Russia that I mounted

the stoop of the Cahoon residence one December evening, pains-
takingly groomed for the soirée Celia had bidden me to. In both
dress and deportment, I was patterning myself after Wallace Reid,
the brightest star in my movie galaxy; I wore a yellow butterfly
bow and a wasp-waisted tweed suit with globular leather buttons, my hair (modishly parted in the middle) exuded a paralyz-
ing scent of bay rum, and my swagger was debonair to the point
where I was having trouble retaining my balance. Whom Celia
was impersonating at the moment I have no idea, but I remember
bee-stung lips pouting out of a heavy mask of rice powder, and a
hairdress of those unlovely puffs we used to call "cootie garages,"
accentuated by a wicked spit curl. The lights in the parlor were
low, and another couple, also from our class, was executing a
vertiginous tango to "La Veeda." While Celia hastened to fetch
me a glass of some ghastly punch made of muscatel and sliced
oranges, I adopted a *dégagé* pose on the arm of a Morris chair and,
stifling a well-bred yawn, covertly studied my surroundings. The
family's taste in art was plainly cultivated; in addition to the standard chromo of Landseer's "Dignity and Impudence," there was a
side elevation of a pearly nude with red hair by Henner and half a
dozen etchings by Anders Zorn. Their library also hinted at a wide
intellectual horizon, ranging from fluff by Peter B. Kyne and James
Oliver Curwood to substantial works by John Spargo and Brand
Whitlock.

"Now, don't be an old bookworm," said Celia effervescently,
seizing my wrist. "Come on, slowpoke, let's shake a tibia!" To be
in close proximity to the figure I had so long admired was an exhil-
arating experience, and when my hostess coyly disclosed that her
folks would not be home until midmorning, I figured I had hit

the mother lode. As the punch took effect, the pace grew mark-edly giddier; there was a rare amount of tickling and squealing, and the ladies had frequent recourse to the lipstick that dangled from the chain of the floor lamp—a fribble that I pretended to sneer at but that actually impressed me as the acme of sophistica-tion. But whatever the romp I contemplated in the Elysian fields, the gods had ordained otherwise. Made overconfident by wine, I decided to re-enact an adagio Wallace Reid had performed in his latest vehicle, *The Dancin' Fool.* I clasped Celia in a cheek-to-cheek embrace and, to the cadences of Coon-Sanders and their Black-hawk orchestra, began a series of improvised pirouettes in the style known as the balconade. Just as we were completing a diz-zying backward dip, my partner's heel caught in the green plush portieres suspended from an archway, and we fell heavily, demol-ishing a rubber plant and the lower panel of a Globe-Wernicke bookcase. At that instant, the door opened and two old crabs by the name of Cahoon entered. They had unexpectedly altered their plans, and, it shortly transpired, my own.

Normally, nothing could have persuaded me to revive such pain-ful memories, but they crowded in pell-mell to a screening I was granted recently, by the Museum of Modern Art, of this very Wallace Reid classic. Like *The Roaring Road* and *Excuse My Dust,* his automotive sagas of the same epoch, *The Dancin' Fool* was a breezy success story, altogether synthetic and as devoid of moti-vation as Happy Hooligan. Its leading man, for all his dazzle, was probably the least gifted actor of the century—a sizable achieve-ment in a medium that begot Nelson Eddy, Henry Wilcoxon, and Mario Lanza. At the risk of alienating readers wholesale, I submit a précis of the plot, but it must be understood that I act merely as an intermediary, or vector. The management will not be responsible for any lost illusions, heartbreak, or ennui poisoning.

The Jones Jug Company, the setting of Wally's initial exploits, is an old-fashioned pottery concern headed by his Uncle Enoch (Raymond Hatton), a stereotyped curmudgeon who bitterly resents progress. Into this milieu bounces Reid, cast as a fresh young hayseed named Sylvester Tibble (or Ves Tibble, naturally), seeking a business career. Given the post of office boy, he at once pantomimes cyclonic energy, raising clouds of dust with his broom, ruffling the bookkeeper's wig, scoffing at the filing system, and generally roiling his elders. After dusk, his uncontrollable zest for dancing leads him into a basement cabaret whose songstress, Junie Budd (Bebe Daniels), seeks his protection from a masher. Wally flattens the offender, and Junie, captivated by his dimples, invites him to her mother's boarding house and offers to coach him in ballroom technique. "You've got regular rattleboxes in your feet," she declares, obviously unaware of a pair that were making every cake-eater in Rhode Island drool with envy. In no time at all—one lap dissolve, in fact—the couple have blossomed out as a dance team in the cabaret, doing a Dutch specialty at their *première* that establishes new frontiers in bathos. Among the patrons, it just so happens, is a wealthy pottery tycoon named Harkins (Tully Marshall), who is established as avid to gain control of the Jones Jug Company's clay pit, a circumstance without burning relevance to the floor show but that provides a yeast for future villainy. Wally and Junie now reappear in an apache number so sensational, presumably, that a rival café owner signs them up at two hundred a week, whereupon they run home to apprise Junie's mother of their success and Wally proposes to her. To

Junie, that is, not her mother, although actually it wouldn't have made much difference. By this point in the proceedings, it was crystal-clear to me that the engineer was drunk in the cab, the locomotive out of control, and the switches wide-open.

At the Jones Jug Company, where our hero continues as office boy while dancing professionally at night—a movie premise as plausible as most of them—the firm's drummer, a blowhard and wineskin, returns from a sales trip and angrily resigns when Wally questions his expense account. Thereupon, in a comic routine that has begun to lose some of its sizzle with repetition, Uncle Enoch upbraids his nephew for exceeding authority, fires him summarily, and hires him back at once. Disclosed next are Junie and Wally at their cabaret that evening, clad in leopard skins and presenting a divertissement billed as "Antediluvian Antics," which it would be flattery to describe as the nadir of choreography in our time. Nonetheless, Harkins (who apparently uses the crib as his headquarters) applauds it vociferously from ringside and invites Wally to his table. There the latter overhears him confide to a subordinate, "The way to get old Jones's business is to buy up his pottery, and I believe he'd sell out for a dollar." Sensing the machinations that threaten his uncle, Wally racks his brain for some novelty that might stimulate sales, and evolves a repulsive line of containers with human faces he calls B-Jones B-Jugs. Uncle Enoch, betraying the one flicker of taste visible anywhere in the picture, quite properly refuses to countenance them, but, to rid himself of Wally's paranoid schemes, permits him to take over as traveling salesman. When Junie discovers her partner has doffed his leotards for commerce, she breaks their engagement in the best musical-comedy tradition, and Wally, approximately as grief-stricken as if a caraway seed had lodged in his teeth, exits

nonchalantly to pursue his destiny. The temptation to emulate him pierced me like a knife. I half rose from my chair; then,
detecting the projectionist's baleful eye fixed on me through the
peephole of his booth, I twisted my features into a sickly placatory
grin and sank back, resigned to perishing like a rat in a trap.

In the ensuing reel, Harkins, repeatedly bilked in his attempts
to flimflam Uncle Enoch out of his pit, cunningly decides to show
the old gentleman the fleshpots, and inveigles him to dinner at
the cabaret. Junie has meanwhile found herself another dancing
partner, though still torchy for the Ragtime Kid. The evening the
new team is unveiled, Wally bursts in unexpectedly—unexpected
by the washroom boy, it would seem, for nobody else exhibits surprise—and, shouldering aside the interloper, struts a duet with
Junie to universal acclaim. Uncle Enoch fumbles on his glasses,
recognizes his scapegrace nephew, and once again thunders,
"You're fired!" By some process of reasoning I was too dense to
comprehend, the revelation that he had been nurturing a gigolo
determines Uncle Enoch to sell out to Harkins. The two retire to
a banquet room to sign the necessary papers; there is the usual
zabaione of misgivings, phony legalities, and the fountain pen that
runs dry, and inevitably Wally comes bounding in with the cornu-
copia of orders he has garnered for B-Jones B-Jugs. Uncle Enoch,
exuberant, makes him a full partner on the spot, and his compet-
itor, after a token display of pique, proves that he has a heart of
gold under his knavish exterior. "We're beaten. It serves us right,"
he says sheepishly. "All along we've been calling him a dancin' fool
and really he's a commercial whiz." The butchery terminates with
Wally imprinting a peck on his sweetheart's cheek and declaring,
with a brisk insincerity guaranteed to reassure his female fans,

"B'gosh, you're going to be my little B'Junie, and b'join the B'Jug family."

You might suppose that a victim of such cinematic mayhem would excite some measure of pity, and that when I reeled out into Fifty-third Street and collided with a pair of elderly dragons laden with Christmas shopping, I would have been accorded a helping hand. On the contrary, both ladies recoiled and gaped at me as though I were aswarm with caterpillars. "Well!" snapped one of them, pursing her lips. "Pickled in the middle of the afternoon, and in a museum, too. I always wondered what went on in there."

I removed my Borsalino and gave her as courteous a bow as I could muster. "If I told you what went on in there, Medusa," I said, "those dentures would drop out of your head. Did you ever hear of a dancing salesman named Ves Tibble—I mean an office boy called Wallace Reid?" Before I could adumbrate the plot, the two of them turned tail and streaked for Fifth Avenue. I worked over toward Sixth, found myself a cool, dark clinic with a sympathetic interne, and eventually managed to justify their diagnosis. What the hell, you might as well be hung for a sheep as for a lamb.

"M" Is for the Migraine
That She Gave Me

IF, IN the tradition of *Asmodeus, or The Devil on Two Sticks*, you and the Prince of Darkness had happened to be flapping around over Sheridan Square one chill December evening in 1925, rubbering down at the human spectacle below, you might have seen the present writer bent over a drawing board in his hall bedroom, laboriously inking in a comic sketch. It portrayed a distraught gentleman careering into a doctor's office, clutching a friend by the wrist and whimpering, "I've got Bright's disease and he has mine." How I had gravitated into this seedy locale, to subsist meanly on a pittance from a humorous weekly that rejected everything I drew, is not especially germane, yet, by and large, my lot did not seem to me insupportable. The temperature of the cubicle was subarctic, the pens and brushes kept fouling in the quilt draped over my head, and a week thence I was fated to collapse with scurvy from living exclusively on crullers, but I hummed a little song as I worked. Parnassus, I had convinced myself by incredible sophistry, was just over the next rise, and my tendons were not even fluttering.

At any rate, I had blown a layer of fixative over my handiwork and was holding it off at arm's length to admire it when I heard the sound of a woman's sobs issuing through the wall of the room adjoining. So piercing was her woe, fraught with such immediacy and heartbreak, that I sat aghast. The voice, I knew, was that of Ivy Spicer, a chlorotic, auburn-haired graduate of Mount Hol–yoke who earned her cakes editing the society page of a Newark morning newspaper and wrote alexandrines on the side. In our few encounters, I had found her pretentious, too often addicted to the Gioconda smile and the quotation from James Elroy Flecker, but she was obviously *in extremis* now and I reacted as Jeffery Far-nol would have wanted me to. Sprinting out into the hall, I beat a hasty tattoo on her door and entered. Ivy, enveloped in a Japanese kimono and obi that had probably belonged to Lafcadio Hearn, lay sprawled on a day bed, weeping convulsively. The candlelit room was heavy with the odor of sandalwood and there was no lack of icons.

"G-go way," she snuffled in response to my overtures. "You're a nasty little hypocrite, like all the rest of them." Interpreting her words as those of a woman betrayed, I declared with as much dignity as the quilt over my head permitted that I, for one, was not given to seducing ladies and abandoning them. Instantly, Ivy's sorrow changed to exasperation. "What are you foomphet-ing about, you idiot?" she snarled. "I'm not crying over any man. I just saw *Stella Dallas*." She then made it clear, as if addressing a Queensland aborigine, that the movie of that title, unknown to me, was a masterpiece second only to the *Götterdämmerung*, and its star, Belle Bennett, the greatest tragedienne since Clara Kimball Young. Luckily, before she could recount the plot some sixth sense warned our landlady, an incorrigible snooper, that two lodgers of opposite sex were fraternizing abovestairs behind a closed door, and she began ululating outside. I made my retreat by the fire escape, and subsequently, when I could afford a visa to cross Fourteenth Street, went to see the picture. Its effect, I had to admit, was cataclysmic. Blinded by scalding tears, I groped my way downtown and confessed to Ivy that she was right. I got precisely what I deserved. She deadpanned me, and, observing that my taste was execrable, enjoined me to read James Elroy Flecker.

As one way of outwitting bailiffs and remaining incommunicado for a spell from the tensions of existence, I recently slipped into a projection room at the Museum of Modern Art, where, by a coincidence, *Stella Dallas* was being screened. Lacking a notebook, I jotted down on the film curator's collar some memoranda which he has kindly allowed me to transcribe before sending it to the Chinaman. If they seem slightly incoherent, I can only plead that they were written in the dark on a slick celluloid surface and that the wearer kept squirming around in the most inexplicable fashion. Perhaps he had caught his pinkie in the spring mechanism of his chair, or possibly he had seen the picture before. It comes to about the same thing.

Ostensibly, *Stella Dallas* treats of mother love and the tremendous self-sacrifice it is legendarily capable of; actually, it is the story—told with a degree of mawkishness such as only three virtuosi of bathos like Samuel Goldwyn, Henry King, and Frances Marion were capable of—of a vulgar, ostentatious woman who bedevils her husband and daughter so relentlessly that she loses them both. Unfortunately, whatever twisted satisfaction one might derive from this payoff cancels out, since the husband is a prig and the daughter a snob. If any movie ever had a more offensive set of characters than *Stella Dallas*, I'd like to know its name. No, I wouldn't, really. I just said that out of nervousness.

Stephen Dallas (Ronald Colman), a pharisaical young squirt with the visage of a plaster saint, has been in love since childhood with Helen Dane (Alice Joyce), one of those unbearable girls whose faces are always transfigured by an inner radiance. (Any enlightened premedical student knows that this condition stems from a disordered bile duct, but no matter.) When Stephen's father is detected in embezzlement, and suicides, the son flees to an obscure mill town and there succumbs to the wiles of a frivolous, rather sluttish creature named Stella Martin (Belle Bennett). Soon after their marriage and the birth of a daughter, Stella develops social ambitions and a taste for gaudy clothes that pain Stephen immeasurably. While he pursues his legal duties at the plant, we see her at the country club sipping tea with a group of matrons whose genteel derision she excites by her extravagant ostrich plumes and killing manner. To make matters worse, she openly hobnobs with Eddie Munn, the club's riding master (Jean Hersholt), a greasy and overaffable tinhorn shunned by the ladies. Eddie's buffooneries—he drolly pretends to swallow a table knife, advertising the feat as "a little parlor trick Eve tried on Adam's apple"—horrify the gathering, but Stella thinks him beguiling and invites him home to dinner. They have uncorked a bottle of beer and are very much *en famille* when Stephen comes in from work. His sniffish displeasure at seeing a stranger posturing about in his wife's hat eventually penetrates to Eddie. "Well," remarks the latter, sheepishly resuming his jacket, "like the roof says to the cyclone, I'm off now." In the domestic squabble that ensues, Stephen involuntarily provokes a tantrum from Stella by announcing his transfer to New York. She refuses to accompany him; they wrangle about the custody of the infant, a curious diversion considering that it is patently a doll rented by Mr. Goldwyn for the occasion, and finally Stella wins the little effigy on the understanding that she will bring it to New York at some undisclosed date. At about this juncture, the curator I was scribbling on lit a match, which struck me as temerity in a man with a celluloid collar, and I had a moment of anxiety for my notes. However, nothing untoward happened, and shortly both of us were again nodding to the hypnotic drone of the projector.

The next couple of reels are a somnambulistic exposition of the child's girlhood; Stella, progressively blowzier and more enamored of Eddie Munn, vegetates in the small town, but her daughter Laurel (Lois Moran) regards her mother's suitor as intolerably boorish and pines for Stephen. Her tenth birthday is ruined by her expulsion from Miss Philiburn's private school, the headmistress having followed Stella and Eddie to New York and seen them enter an unsavory rooming house. Needless to say, they are guiltless of wrongdoing, and the scene in which Laurel and her mother await the guests who never arrive is a sentimental holocaust on a par with the death of Little Nell. I had a strong impulse to blubber, and let me tell you, Dick, I don't blubber easily. Stephen Dallas, meanwhile, has rediscovered Helen, his early flame, now a widow with three sons, and is pressing Stella for a divorce. She has broken with Eddie, by this time a decrepit wino who shambles about chewing a bunch of scallions for some arcane low-comedy reason, and she clings obstinately to her marital status, fearful that Laurel may throw in with her father. Eight or nine years pass in this gloomy state of emotional disequilibrium, and then, at a spa, the girl falls head over heels for a blueblood named Richard

Grosvenor, played in his most whippy vein by Douglas Fairbanks, Jr. Their exquisite rapport—dramatized in a febrile montage of tennis, hiking, and various aquatic sports under the caption "Days that flew on swallows' wings"—is short-lived; mortified by Stella's parvenu clothes and deportment, Laurel precipitately terminates their stay. Homeward bound on the train, Stella by chance overhears several women chuckling over her deficiencies, cruelly referring to her as a millstone around Laurel's neck and a major obstacle to Grosvenor's marrying her. Comes now the actor's dream, the big obligatory scene of self-abnegation as Stella seeks out Helen Morrison and, amid more nose-blowing than a school of sperm whales, begs her to wed Stephen and adopt Laurel. "I couldn't rob a mother of her only little girl," Helen protests, all swollen with nobility like Bertha Kalich. Whether from Helen's proximity or because her own bile duct is beginning to kick up, Stella's face becomes transfigured with that old inner radiance. "But you don't understand, Mrs. Morrison, I've thought it all out," she implores. "When you get married, your name will be Mrs. Dallas, too, and when Laurel gets married, the wedding invitations will read right. I'd like people to think she's yours. You're the kind of a mother she could be proud of. I—I ain't. She'll never be nobody, Mrs. Morrison, with me shackled around one foot." Well, sir, you can imagine the weeping and the kissing and the slobbering this brings on. And as though it weren't gruesome enough, they have to top it with a shot of Stella pausing impulsively at a bouquet, asking "May I take a rose to remember you by?" and imprinting a kiss on the bolster of the bed Laurel is to occupy. I vum, it makes a man come all over queasy.

In case anybody thinks these lachrymose doings prefigure a squeeze, though, he doesn't know a false climax when he sees one. After Stephen and Helen have been united in what looks like a warehouse for aging bourbon, Laurel comes to stay with them and inadvertently learns of Stella's sacrifice. She returns to the maternal roof, and, as hallowed movie custom requires, keels over with brain fever. While wielding a palmetto fan at her bedside, a peerless method of inducing pneumonia in an invalid, her mother peeks into Laurel's diary and discovers she still languishes after Richard Grosvenor but fears the union to be hopeless on account of Stella. Why she doesn't strangle the brat then and there is unclear, except that it presents a juicy opportunity for further histrionics. She seeks out Eddie Munn, who has drunk himself into oblivion, peremptorily declares her intention of marrying him, and abstracts one of his early photographs. She then hastens back to apprise Laurel of her impending nuptials, feigning immense exuberance and cooing sticky endearments to Eddie's picture. The stratagem succeeds; Laurel hurtles back to Stephen and his family, and there is an orgy of reconciliation, climaxed by the reappearance of Richard—an older, more understanding Richard, with a new dignity about him. This time he has a mustache.

The closing section of *Stella Dallas* is, I suppose, more familiar to more people on the weather side of forty than "Tipperary." The mansion ablaze with lights on the night of Laurel's wedding, the throng clustered outside in the rain-swept street, and finally Stella, in sodden rags held together by a giant safety pin, clinging to the fence and yearning upward for a last glimpse of her child—boy, that's catharsis like Mother used to make. The beating Sam Goldwyn inflicted on his heroine and his audience surpassed anything that Gus Flaubert ever did to Emma Bovary. He gave anguish a new dimension, lifted nausea into another sphere, with the juxtaposed shot of the bride nearing the altar on her father's arm and Stella being pried away from the gate by an inexorable policeman. "I'm going," ran the immortal subtitle. "I was only seeing how pretty the young lady was." No restorative in the world can counteract the effect of a line like that, except maybe a cherry smash.

Like a delayed-action mine, however, the full impact of the picture did not hit me until hours later—dinnertime, to be exact. In the role of paterfamilias, which I play with considerable *brio*, I was carving a Smithfield ham and suddenly found that I needed an extra plate for the nubbins. Without slackening rhythm, I directed a fifteen-year-old baggage on my right, currently home from boarding school, to fetch it from the kitchen. At least thirty seconds passed while Sleeping Beauty sat gaping at the ham, her thoughts far away. I ripped out a more forcible command, couched in the idiom of the quarterdeck. "I'm going," she said resentfully. "I was only seeing how pretty the cloves were." The cadence of her words sharply evoked all the misery I had been closeted with that afternoon; I let fall the cutlery and, burying my face in the crook of my elbow, broke down.

The baggage stared at me mystified. "What's wrong with *him*?" she asked her mother. "Is he jingled?"

"No more than usual," said the mem kindly. "Probably been nosing around a film vault again. Eat your squash."

In a short while, I was right as rain again and had everybody in a roar pretending to swallow a table knife. It's a trick I picked up from some movie or other whose name escapes me. If you think of it, do me a favor, will you? Thank you.

Mayfair Mama,
Turn Your Damper Down

THE second-class-passenger complement of the S. S. *Leviathan*, eastbound for Cherbourg in June, 1927, included some rare birds. There was an opulent Frenchwoman of a certain age on whom Toulouse-Lautrec had reputedly squandered his patrimony, a Belgian bicycle team fresh from the six-day races at the Garden, an elderly dandy of the era of Berry Wall who claimed to have had more than a waltzing acquaintance with the Jersey Lily, and a Greek gem dealer with a black monocle and a Malacca stick containing a handful of uncut diamonds. At least, he *said* they were diamonds, and I, dizzied by my first trip abroad and saturated with Maurice Dekobra's *The Madonna of the Sleeping Cars*, joyously accepted his confidence. I doubt whether anyone else so rabid for adventure has ever embarked on a maiden voyage to Europe. I was ready for every contingency—international cardsharps, dacoits, and, particularly, veiled charmers with mocking mouths who might entice me to Salonika. Folded at the bottom of my suitcase, where they could be easily stolen, were blueprints of a mitrailleuse I had cooked up, together with a trench coat suitable for tracking the culprits through the purlieus of Stambul. I sat in the smoking lounge of the ocean greyhound expelling thin jets of Turkish from my nostrils until my head rang like a burglar alarm. I cultivated a hooded, watchful gaze.

Contrary to the hopes inspired by Dekobra's novel, almost nothing happened to me on the crossing, and when it did, it was of a completely unexpected nature. The second day out, a gusty, obstreperous party named Lightfoot was moved into my cabin. He was a man of shattering vitality, a combination of Olsen and Johnson, with an explosive guffaw that set the lifeboats quivering in their davits. A compulsive talker in the great tradition, Lightfoot instantly peppered me with his history and aspirations, downing a hogshead of bourbon meanwhile. He had been a World War ace, he told me, and was currently en route to Le Bourget, from which he proposed to fly the Atlantic solo. He predicted that this would overshadow Lindy's feat, and I agreed unequivocally, since he made no mention of using an airplane for the hop.

Time has mercifully dimmed the memory of our association during the next five days, but one episode remains untarnished. Lightfoot and I occupied a table in the dining saloon with a mousy schoolteacher from South Braintree—a Miss Purvis—and a fattish, mealy androgyne called Rossiter, who was going to the Hook of Holland to study counterpoint. Lightfoot promptly dedicated himself to making Rossiter's life a burden. He lay awake nights contriving practical jokes to play on the musician, each more barbarous than the last. They reached their climax one noon when Rossiter was late for luncheon. Adjuring us to secrecy, Lightfoot produced a baking-powder biscuit of sponge rubber, one of those realistic facsimiles sold in magic-supply shops. I presume it was part of his traveling kit, for, well equipped as the *Leviathan* was, it carried no gear of that kind. He then smothered it in sauce, dabbed sauce on our three plates for authenticity, and gleefully awaited Rossiter. The latter, his appetite sharpened by a turn around the deck, sat down and addressed the hors-d'œuvre with relish. As his fork pressed into the biscuit, it discharged a mournful squeal that short-circuited conversation all over the room. People half rose, craning their necks and peering spellbound at Rossiter. Apparently unable to credit his ears, he again cut into the biscuit, and again the hidden mechanism responded. In the attendant wave of mirth, cued by Lightfoot's bellow, Rossiter stood up with simple dignity and, I am glad to report, flung the delicacy into his tormentor's face.

The acquisitive instinct dies hard. Pawing over the detritus in my bookshelf latterly, I was confronted after two decades with the very copy of *The Madonna of the Sleeping Cars* that had set me roving. Unlike its owner, its spine was still erect and soldierly and its jacket free of mildew. The temptation to see what sort of tinsel had captivated me at twenty-three, as well as to spend a couple of hours on my shoulder blades, was irresistible. Before you could say Maurice Dekobra, I was in the horizontal, drinking in the stuff in great, thirsty gulps.

The tale M. Dekobra told so artfully that it tore through five editions like a sickle-bar mower was, between ourselves, no trail blazer. The formula of high life and low loins, to borrow Aldous Huxley's apposite phrase, had long been employed by E. Phillips Oppenheim, Paul Morand, and other writers of that genre. Dekobra merely souped it up, adding a high-octane element few novelists had taken advantage of until then—Soviet Russia. There may have been earlier variations on the theme of the Beauty and the Bolshevik, but I venture that there had been none more foolish.

The title of *The Madonna of the Sleeping Cars* prefigures its exotic and shifting locale; the narrative, related by a singular coxcomb named Prince Séliman, veers from London to Berlin, from Vienna to the Caucasus, and from Monaco to Loch Lomond with a breathlessness unmatched outside a *Vogue* fashion forecast. The Prince, a Frenchman whose patent to nobility is never made quite clear, is at the outset footloose in London, recently separated from his wealthy American wife. An advertisement in the personal column of the *Times* secures him a position as private secretary to a lovely gadabout widow called Lady Diana Wynham. "In Paris," observes Dekobra as he proceeds to describe her high cheekbones, sensual lips, and limpid eyes, "there is a saying that when an Englishwoman is beautiful she is very beautiful." Trust the French to coin a nifty like that; no wonder they produced Voltaire. At any rate, the comely peeress has earned an international reputation for audacity and chic. She shyly confesses that "there is not a customs officer in any country who doesn't recognize the perfume of my valises, and who doesn't know the most sacred details of my lingerie." Having spent the better part of two million pounds since her husband's death, she feels she needs a cool head to counsel her, and offers Prince Séliman five hundred pounds a month to do so. He takes the post but spurns the money, declaring he wishes only relief from boredom: "I don't rent my services, I give them." At twenty-three, I understood his motives perfectly; I had done the same kind of thing on innumerable occasions. Today, I incline to sleep on it.

One of the Prince's first assignments is to conduct Lady Diana to a session with a celebrated psychologist, Professor Siegfried Traurig, to have a dream of hers interpreted. The reader gets a foretaste here of Dekobra's love of the salty simile, a passion that is to boil over later, when he speaks of "those European clinics where they dig up the soul with the shovel of introspection and where they slice apart the elements of the will with the chisel of psychopathic analysis." Equally poetic figures are evoked, farther on, by a description of a caviar binge ("As the lemon wept acid tears on the delicacy, etc.") and by Lady Diana's treatment of a lover ("I . . . put my guest under the cold shower-bath of refusal and then on the burning flame of hope"). Subsequently, in a petulant mood, she excoriates the Prince for his horrid logic, "which inevitably throws the wild horses of imagination with its lasso." It is significant that once the steeds start bucking, Dekobra himself conveniently mislays that old riata.

To continue: Professor Traurig elicits the details of Lady Diana's dream, orders the Prince to kiss her, and photographs what is represented to be a spectral analysis of her reactions—standard psychoanalytical technique, as any fool knows. The basic test reveals that she has a perfection neurosis, which one presumes will yield to a little snake oil, and our heroine blithely goes her way. The plot now starts bubbling in the percolator. Rumor spreads that Sumatra-rubber stocks, her ladyship's chief investment, are shaky, and tradespeople begin to dun her. Seeking to divert their attention momentarily, Lady Diana causes a scandal, by executing a shocking dance at a charity matinée. Her costume will be helpful to those in a tight financial spot. It consists of "a *cache-sexe* no bigger than the hand of a sacristan and held in place by an almost invisible garland of bindweed, two buskins with silver ribbons, and a veil of white mousseline which hung down to her elbows." Of course, if you live in an area where sacristans and bindweed are unobtainable, you will simply have to improvise, but anybody with an ounce of initiative can make do.

The chandeliers have hardly ceased rocking before Lady Diana has another brainstorm. Fifteen thousand acres of oil lands near Telav, on the Black Sea, formerly owned by her hubby, have been nationalized by the Bolsheviks. However, she has information that the Soviet delegate to Berlin, Leonid Varichkine, can be bribed into allowing her to exploit them. Prince Séliman departs forthwith to brace him. At the Walhalla Restaurant, in Bellevuestrasse, he and Varichkine, a smooth apple in Bond Street clothes, get together over half a dozen 1911 Heidsieck Monopole. The Russian knows what he wants, and it isn't petroleum: "I'll countersign the papers for her concession when the rising sun surprises her in my arms." In the higher echelons, obviously, proposals of the sort are a commonplace; Séliman, unruffled, wires his principal, and she arrives to look Varichkine over. In the meantime, another, and sinister, character has entered the wings—Mme. Irina Mouravieff, the delegate's mistress and herself a power with the Politburo. She tacks up a "No Poaching" sign, accompanied by dire threats. Everybody, naturally, ignores her caveat; and understandably, because otherwise the chlorophyll would drain out of the story. Varichkine, in fact, is so smitten with Lady Diana that he offers his hand, and she, attracted by the uproar the marriage would excite in Berkeley Square, accepts it. The round ends with Mme. Mouravieff darkly promising the Prince, who she feels is in some way culpable, that he will rue the day. He counters with an epigram, shaped like a cheese blintz, to the effect that "a man who is warned is worth two ordinary men." As events prove, he would have done better to stow the bravado and tighten up his accident policy.

Reduced to essentials, the rest of the yarn treats of Mme. Mouravieff's revenge. She lures the Prince to Nikolaïa, in the Caucasus, to inspect the oil lands, by trailing before him a cuddly *Mädchen* named Klara, with a mutinous nose and a mole on her cheekbone. Séliman and Klara flirt their way into the swansdown in Vienna, and in Constantinople, weakened by raisins, she acknowledges being a Russian agent and warns him to turn back. He takes ship for Batum nevertheless, and at Trebizond encounters another obstacle—his wife, Griselda, cruising aboard her yacht with friends. They exchange sighs over bygone ecstasies, seem about to become reconciled, and then hearken to the plot, which beckons the Prince on to Muscovy. Shortly after he reaches Nikolaïa, the trap is sprung, and he lands in an underground cell operated by the Cheka.

The idiom thereafter, up to the time the Prince escapes on his wife's yacht, has been made tolerably familiar by such savants as Eugene Lyons and George Sokolsky. I shall not queer their pitch beyond saying that Dekobra, too, is a pretty deft man with a Red atrocity. Mme. Mouravieff is, of course, on hand at all hours to chivy and gloat, but the Prince finally slips his leash. Off the Riviera, he and his wife adjust their differences, a minor climax preceding a whirlwind finish at Castle Glensloy, in Scotland. Here the jealous Russky hunts down Lady Diana ("Two tigresses facing one another. The daughter of the Mongols against the daughter of the Celts. Two races. Two worlds. . . . Above all, two women"), draws a heater on her rival, and is pistoled by Varichkine. The curtain rings down on Milady bidding adieu to her devoted secretary at the Gare de l'Est as the Orient Express snorts impatiently in the background. She has brushed off Varichkine and is faring forth in quest of someone "who will cater to my whims and ripen in my safe-deposit box some golden apples from the garden of Hesperides." Which, let us fervently hope, she will pare with the platinum fruit knife of restraint.

No doubt my senses were sharpened razor-keen by contact with the world of intrigue and counterplot, because just as I closed *The Madonna of the Sleeping Cars* I detected a soft footfall outside my room and the sound of the doorknob being tried gently. In a flash, I realized that it was my family, come to spy on my movements. Quick as a cat, I popped the book into my jumper, removed my teeth, and pretended to be deep in slumber when they entered. It was a close shave, for had they caught me, I would have had short shrift. This way, I have not only long shrift but Dekobra—and, baby, that's enough to make anybody's cup run over.

Hungarian Goulash,
with Battered Noodles

WHY the memory of a screen actress named Constance Talmadge should cause, after two highballs and three decades, a
constriction in the throat and misty vision is something I can't
readily explain. I suppose it is one of those idiosyncrasies I must
accept as normal nowadays, along with progressive penury and
the vertigo that attends lacing my shoes. Though I realize such
belated homage crackles like a paper of ancient snuff, I may as
well 'fess up that yesteryear I was spoony over Miss Talmadge to
the point of idolatry. I wallowed in every picture, major or minor,
she deigned to appear in, and, when called upon, could instantly
furnish authoritative data on her birthstone, favorite flower, and
bust measurement. It seems singular, therefore, that with such a
financial and emotional investment in this quicksilver creature,
the only movie of hers I could recall until recently was a boudoir
farce called *The Duchess of Buffalo*, and that merely because of the
circumstances under which I first saw it. One autumn afternoon
in 1926, I dropped in to visit a former college classmate of mine,
Steamy Welch, who was employed as a copywriter in some vast
advertising agency near Grand Central. Steamy, said my infor-

mants, was the coming man in the agency, an embryonic tycoon, and it sounded credible; he had been a big wheel under the elms, a miracle of scholarship and co-ordination, and classified, in the jargon then stylish, as a snake, or suave operator with the ladies. I still retain a clear image of him at a Junior Week tea dance, clad in a four-button jacket of unbleached sisal and pants with twenty-two-inch bottoms, expertly weaving his partner through the intricacies of the toddle. The orchestra, full of saxophones and tenor banjos, was playing either "Dardanella" or "Wildflower," and when Steamy whirled to complete an arabesque, you caught the glint of an octavo-size metal flask in his hip pocket. There were no flies on Steamy.

At any rate, I found my schoolfellow in one of a maze of tiny glass cubicles, moodily biting his knuckles and trying to evolve some dithyrambs for a process cheese. He hailed me effusively and confirmed the rumors of his success. He was now earning a salary well in excess of twenty thousand a year—without bonuses, of course—and expected to be made vice-president of the firm shortly. He had just acquired a Spanish hacienda at Rye, in the yacht basin of which he proposed to moor a forty-five-foot yawl. Actually, he confessed wryly, he never knew a moment's leisure; all manner of pestilential bores like Charlie Schwab and Eugene Grace kept badgering him for advice on their securities, and he was debating the idea of leasing a grouse preserve in Scotland as a way of escaping them. Did I have any more cogent suggestion, he asked with appealing candor. Just as I was studying the problem, the door flew open and a forthright gentleman entered without bothering to remove his hat.

"Hi ya, Welch," he said, consulting a notebook. "You're two months behind on that suit of clothes. Cough up a double sawbuck or we'll hang a judgment on you." As my friend, glowing like a bed of phlox, slowly fished out his wallet, his nemesis scrawled a receipt and gave him a short, incisive lecture on the ethics of installment buying. When he had departed, Steamy looked so shopworn that I suggested a small libation on the altar of Silenus. Three or four shells of needle beer restored his *amour-propre*, and by easy stages we gained a Hungarian restaurant in Yorkville, where I remember downing a great deal of synthetic Tokay and dancing a czardas in a rather abandoned fashion. There was a fuzzy interval outside a phone booth while Steamy vainly besought two nurses on Staten Island to join us in making whoopee, and then I was in a neighborhood movie house, blinking ponderously at Miss Talmadge's antics and wondering how a film called *The Duchess of Buffalo* came to be laid in Russia. Steamy had vanished to fulfill his portion, which, the last time I heard, was managing a lubritorium outside Spearfish, South Dakota.

A few days ago, while peaceably traversing West Fifty-third Street, I was set upon by a hooded trio lurking in the entresol of the Museum of Modern Art, forced at pistol point upstairs into the film library's projection room, and compelled to see *The Duchess of Buffalo* again. The press gang gave no clue to its motives in shanghaiing me, but it was made clear that I could expect reprisals against my loved ones should I fail to report my findings. If, consequently, an apprehensive note steals into the following recapitulation from time to time, the reader will understand I speak under duress. Here and there, from sentences patently meant to be read backward, he will glean some conception of the ordeal I underwent. Honestly, my hand still shakes whenever I light up a strip of film.

Hungarian playwrights always having been pre-eminent in the field of laborious fun, *The Duchess of Buffalo* was derived from a piece written by two Hungarian playwrights and adapted for the screen by a third. The megaphone and the production reins were handled by two local boys named, respectively, Sidney Franklin and Joseph M. Schenck, but their contribution was so much of a piece with the authors' that if I were aedile, I would have conferred honorary Hungarian citizenship on them. As for the cast supporting Miss Talmadge, it was nothing if not cosmopolitan—Tullio Carminati, Edward Martindale, Rose Dionne, Chester Conklin, and Jean de Briac, all of them gustily impersonating Russians of every degree of eminence from Grand Duke to hotelkeeper. Mistaken identity, of course, was the theme, and it was exploited with such tenacity that for seventy minutes the chills never stopped rippling down my spine. To be sure, the gun that was kept pressed against it throughout didn't help any.

The plot of *The Duchess of Buffalo*, woven of summerweight thistledown, concerns the obstacles surmounted by a wellborn young dragoon, Lieutenant Orloff (Carminati), in wedding Marian Duncan, an American ballerina from Buffalo (Miss Talmadge). As we fade in on the latter's triumphant recital before an audience of St. Petersburg swells, the opening title sets the mood: "Marian Duncan danced in America with a veil. Then she tried Russia without a veil, and oh boy-ovitch. She was so good that two visiting Scotchmen forgot their change at the box-office." One gathers from the spectacle onstage, which resembles a spring pageant in the secondary schools, that the Muscovites are ravenous for entertainment, but it presently develops that Marian is the magnet of every eye, and in particular that of a seasoned voluptuary named the Grand Duke Gregory Alexandrovitch (Edward

Martindale). His surreptitious ogling and mustache-twirling, under the very nose of the jealous Grand Duchess Olga Petrovna (Rose Dionne), are guaranteed to tickle anyone's risibilities—save those, possibly, of a man with a Colt in his back—and the camera now leaps to another spectator, even more deeply interested, Marian's lieutenant. Orloff, a dashing youngster from the tips of his well-polished boots to his paleolithic forehead, has been chaperoning his ladylove from the wings, tremulous lest she discard her ultimate veil. Fortunately or otherwise, the *corps de ballet* interposes itself as she does, the curtain falls, and, by the time the lovers grapple, Marian's charms have been fireproofed in a baggy leotard clearly improvised from a suit of heavy woolen underwear. In this decent if oppressive garb, she receives from Orloff a ring plighting their troth, and amid protracted twittering the couple finalize plans to marry at once.

As anyone conversant with dragoons is aware, a Russian dragoon desirous of matrimony must first obtain his Grand Duke's consent, so next day, piling Marian into a sleigh, Orloff sets about procuring it. His superior, abstractedly selecting a diamond brooch to be sent to Marian, at first views the petition with favor but, on learning the name of the prospective fiancée, harshly forbids alliance with a dancer. "Then," says Orloff, unbuckling his sword with the *élan* any dragoon worth a hoot in Hollywood would be expected to display, "I must ask to resign my commission."

Well, sir, if there is one art at which a czarist noble excels, it is dealing with insolent puppies. Placing his arms akimbo—the akimbo position is mandatory in all productions budgeted at three hundred dollars or over—Gregory Alexandrovitch icily rejoins, "You are to be detained in your quarters three days. Perhaps you will have changed your mind by then." Marian, meanwhile, has driven home to order dinner. With rare insight into the native character, not to say political clairvoyance, she realizes that once those Russkis get to jawing, a person may as well grab herself a hot meal.

The misunderstandings now begin to sprout like forsythia; the Grand Duke hurries straightway to Marian's scatter, where she tenderly awaits Orloff, in the belief that *he* has sent her the brooch, and there is a passage of kittenish lovemaking to congeal the blood as the two, separated by a folding screen, tickle each other delirious. Eventually, her fingertips surprise his beard—the same classic dénouement in which Charley Chase or Larry Semon discovers he has been stroking a runaway lion—and she is compelled to dampen his ardor without alienating him altogether. The Grand Duke, nevertheless, refuses her entreaties to spare Orloff and exits majestically, not suspecting that Marian, a hoyden to the last, has pinned the brooch to his cape. Incredibly enough, someone neglected to add the obligatory hilarious scene of his wife stumbling on the bauble and foaming like a Seidlitz powder. For an instant, I had a flicker of suspicion about the scenarist's real nationality. Ferenc Molnar never would have muffed an opportunity like that.

Presumably desolated by this impasse, Marian sends word to her lover urging him to forget her and departs for Orel, a step that provokes a wholesale migration to that city. Orloff breaks arrest to follow her, the Grand Duke conceives the notion of renewing his courtship there, and his Duchess, suspecting that he is philandering, decides to pursue and eavesdrop. We thereupon cut to the manager of Orel's leading hotel, Chester Conklin (obviously sheepish about his role in this enterprise), reacting to a telegram reserving space for the Grand Duchess and commanding secrecy.

In the tradition of Hungarian farce, he of course instantly disobeys. He confides the secret to his staff, confuses Marian with the patrician visitor, for no earthly reason, and installs her in the imperial suite. Orloff has meanwhile overtaken Marian and suggests they flee to Paris. Before they can do so, though, the local company of dragoons insists on tendering a banquet in honor of the putative Grand Duchess, which, nobody needs to be told, is the signal for the Grand Duke to step back into the plot. Playing on Marian's fear of exposure—she has used her influence to shield Orloff from arrest—he caddishly enclasps her waist in public and begs indulgence of the officers to retire, as he and his lady are fatigued from their journey. Knowing the monkeyshines this portended, I sagged down in my seat in the projection room with a dolorous sigh, but my escorts were plainly diverted. "Hot spit!" chuckled one of them under his hood. "Let's see you crawl out of *that* one, sister." I hinted, as unobstrusively as I could, that she undoubtedly would. "Shaddap," he ordered, prodding my spine with his roscoe. "Pipe down if yuh know what's good fer yuh." I don't, but I piped.

The sequence that follows is the sort of demented inter-bedroom frolic Avery Hopwood used to write with his left hand while feeding himself aspirin with his right to deaden his sensibilities. The alarums and excursions in the imperial suite, the headlong buffooneries as the Grand Duke and Orloff pop in and out of closets manhandling Marian and evading each other, generate the same cast-iron glee as *Getting Gertie's Garter* and *Up in Mabel's Room*. Whenever my contemporaries are disposed to bemoan the decline of the theater, by the way, they might profitably recall that these high jinks and the dramas of Eugene Walter were the only available pabulum in their youth. Anyhow, at the height of the carnage the real Grand Duchess comes blundering in like a blue-bottle, the lovers manage to smuggle her husband offscene and establish their bona fides, the Grand Duke benevolently excuses Orloff's desertion, and everything ends copacetically with a Greek Orthodox wedding presided over by an archimandrite from the Central Casting Agency.

I fatuously imagined that the psychic welts left by *The Duchess of Buffalo* had subsided until, somewhat later the same day, I stopped by the New York Public Library to renew a card that had lapsed. It must have been a purely instinctive response, but when the clerk demanded my occupational status for the application, I replied, "A hostage."

After a wary silence, during which she pretended to examine my references but actually fumbled for a buzzer under the counter, she cleared her throat. "We don't recognize that as a vocation," she said. "Just what is the nature of your work?"

"Golly, I don't know," I pondered. "I guess you might call me a snapper-up of unconsidered trifles, but right now I'm in jeopardy on account of a movie. You see, it's like this—" Before I could expatiate, a uniformed man with a rather burly neck took me by the collar and guided me to the Forty-second Street exit. All around, a hell of a day, though I have one thing to be thankful for. At least I didn't run into Steamy Welch.

It Takes Two to Tango,
but Only One to Squirm

BY CURRENT standards, the needs of a young man-about-town in Providence, Rhode Island, in 1921 were few—an occasional pack of straw-tipped Melachrinos, an evening of canoeing on the Ten Mile River, with its concomitant aphrodisiac, a pail of chocolate creams, and a mandatory thirty-five cents daily for admission to the movies. My fluctuating resources (most of the family's money evaporated in visionary schemes like a Yiddish musical-comedy production of *The Heart of Midlothian*) often forced me to abjure tobacco and amour, but I would sooner have parted with a lung than missed such epochal attractions as *Tol'able David* or Rudolph Valentino in *The Four Horsemen of the Apocalypse*, and I worked at some very odd jobs indeed to feed my addiction to the cinema. One of them, I recall, was electroplating radiators in a small, dismal factory that turned out automobile parts. It was an inferno of dirt and noise; half a dozen presses, operated by as many scorbutic girls whose only diet seemed to be pork pies, were kept busy turning out the honeycomb radiators used in several cars at that time, and it was my task to baptize these artifacts in a huge vat filled with boiling acid. The fumes that rose from the immersion were so noisome that within a month I lost eleven pounds and developed nightmares during which I shrieked like a brain-fever bird. Compelled under parental pressure to resign, I wheedled a job as clerk at the baked-goods counter of Shepard's, a department store that dealt in fancy groceries. Overnight, my anemia magically vanished. Cramming myself with cinnamon buns, broken cookies, jelly doughnuts, ladyfingers, brownies, macaroons—anything I could filch while the floorwalker's back was turned—I blew up to fearful proportions. When not folding boxes or discomposing customers, I transported fresh stock from the bakery on the top floor of the building, a function that eventually led to my downfall. One afternoon, spying a beguiling tureen, I snatched a heaping ladleful of what I thought was whipped cream but which proved to be marshmallow. Just as I was gagging horribly, I heard behind me the agonized whisper, "Cheese it, here comes Mr. Madigan!" and the floorwalker appeared, his mustache aquiver. He treated me to a baleful scrutiny, inquired whether I was subject to fits, and made a notation on his cuff. The following payday, my envelope contained a slip with a brief, unemotional dispatch. It stated that due to a country-wide shortage of aprons, the company was requisitioning mine and returning me to civilian life.

After a fortnight of leisure, my bloat had disappeared but so had my savings, and, unable to wangle credit or passes from the picture houses, I reluctantly took a job selling vacuum cleaners from door to door. The equipment that graced my particular model must have weighed easily three hundred pounds, and I spent a hideous day struggling on and off streetcars with it and beseeching suburban matrons to hold still for a demonstration. I was met everywhere by a vast apathy, if not open hostility; several prospects, in fact, saw fit to pursue me with brooms. Finally, a young Swedish housewife, too recent an immigrant to peg a tyro, allowed me to enter her bungalow. How I managed to blow all the fuses and scorch her curtains, I have no idea, but it happened in an *Augenblick*. The next thing I knew, I was fleeing through an azalea bed under a hail of Scandinavian cusswords, desperately hugging my appliances and coils of hose. The coup de grâce came upon my return to the warehouse. It transpired I had lost a nozzle and various couplings, elbows, and flanges, the cost of which I had to make good by pawning the household samovar.

It was more or less inevitable these early travails should return from limbo when, as happened recently, I settled myself into a projection room at the Museum of Modern Art with a print of *The Four Horsemen of the Apocalypse*. Actually, I would have much preferred to reinspect another vehicle of Valentino's called B*lood and Sand*, which co-starred Nita Naldi, down whom it used to be my boyhood ambition to coast on a Flexible Flyer, but the ravages of time had overtaken it. (Miss Naldi, *mirabile dictu*, is as symmetrical as ever.) T*he Four Horsemen*, however, provided the great lover with a full gamut for his histrionic talents, and a notable supporting cast, containing, among others, Alice Terry, Wallace Beery, Alan Hale, Stuart Holmes, Joseph Swickard, and Nigel de Brulier. It was difficult to believe that only thirty-two years before—only yesterday, really, I told myself comfortingly—it had kept me on the edge of my chair. Ah, well, the chairs were narrower in those days. You positively get lost in the ones at the Museum.

The Four Horsemen, as any nonagenarian will remember, was based on Vicente Blasco Ibáñez's best seller. It was released on the heels of the First World War, and its pacifist theme was unquestionably responsible for a measure of its success, but Valentino's reptilian charm, his alliances with Winifred Hudnut and Natacha Rambova, the *brouhaha* about his excesses and idiosyncrasies were the real box-office lure. An interminable, narcotic genealogy precedes his appearance in the film, establishing a complex hierarchy of ranchers in the Argentine dominated by his maternal grandfather, an autocratic Spanish hidalgo. Julio Desnoyers (Valentino) is French on his father's side and the patriarch's favorite; he has German cousins being groomed as legatees of the family fortune, and the sequence pullulates with murky domestic intrigue. Petted and indulged by the old man, Julio grows up into a sleek-haired finale hopper who tangos sinuously, puffs smoke into the bodices of singsong girls, and generally qualifies as a libertine. In the fullness of time, or roughly six hundred feet of minutiae that remain a secret between the cameraman and the cutter, Julio's mother inherits half the estate and removes her son, daughter, and husband to Paris, where they take up residence in a Gallic facsimile of Kaliski & Gabay's auction rooms. Julio dabbles at painting—at least, we behold him before an easel in the manner of those penny-arcade tableaux called "What the Butler Saw Through the Keyhole," sighting off lickerishly at some models dressed in cheesecloth—and, in more serious vein, applies himself to seducing Marguerite Laurier (Alice Terry), the wife of a French senator. The role must have been a nerve-racking one for Valentino. Not only did he have to keep an eye peeled for the senator but the production was being directed by Miss Terry's husband-to-be, Rex Ingram. No wonder the poor cuss fell apart when he did.

To provide Valentino with a setting for his adagios, the affair gets under way at a fashionable temple of the dance called the Tango Palace, packed with gigolos and ladies in feathered turbans swaying orgiastically; then Marguerite, apprehensive of gossip, makes surreptitious visits to her lover's atelier. He, intent on steam-rollering her into the Turkish corner, is oblivious of all else, and there is a portentous moment, embroidering the favorite movie thesis that mankind always exhibits unbridled sensuality just prior to Armageddon, when his male secretary tries to show him a newspaper headline reading, "ARCHDUKE FERDINAND ASSASSINATED AT SARAJEVO," only to have Julio petulantly brush it aside. The symbolism now starts to pile up thick and fast. The secretary, croaking ominously, exits to consult a mysterious bearded philosopher in a Russian tunic (Nigel de Brulier), who, it has been planted, dwells upstairs. No reliable clue to this character's identity is anywhere given, but he seems to be a mélange of Prince Myshkin, Savonarola, and Dean Inge, possesses the gift of tongues, and is definitely supernatural. His reaction to the murder is much more immediate, possibly because he doesn't have a girl in his room. "This is the beginning of the end," he declares somberly. "The brand that will set the world ablaze." Downstairs, meanwhile, Marguerite's scruples are melting like hot marzipan under Julio's caresses, and it is manifest that she is breaking up fast. The camera thereupon cuts back to the oracle extracting an apple from a bowl of fruit. "Do you not wonder that the apple, with its coloring, was chosen to represent the forbidden fruit?" he asks the secretary, with a cryptic smile. "But, when peeled, how like woman without her cloak of virtue!" I don't know how this brand of rhetoric affected other people of my generation, but it used to make me whinny. I secretly compared it to the insupportable sweetness of a thousand violins.

Before very long, Marguerite's husband ferrets out her peccadillo, wrathfully announces his intention of divorcing her, and challenges Julio to a duel. The scandal never eventuates, happily; in response to a general mobilization order, the senator joins his regiment, the Fifth Calvados Fusiliers, and his wife, seeking to make atonement for her guilt, enrolls as a nurse. "The flames of war had singed the butterfly's wings," explains a Lardnerian subtitle, "and in its place there was—a woman, awakening to the call of France." Excused from military service because of his nationality, Julio dawdles around Paris making an apathetic pitch for Marguerite, which she priggishly rejects on the ground that venery is unseemly while the caissons roll—a view diametrically opposed to that of another nurse in the same conflict described in *A Farewell to Arms*. Throughout the preceding, the soothsayer in the attic has been relentlessly conjuring up double-exposure shots of the apocalyptic horsemen and their sinister baggage, and a funereal pall descends on the action—not that it has been a Mardi Gras thus far, by any means. Julio's father (Joseph Swickard) has been taken prisoner at his country house by a detachment of uhlans commanded by Wallace Beery, who proceeds to stage one of those classic Hearst-Sunday-supplement revels with bemonocled Prussians singing "*Ach, du lieber Augustin*," girls running around in their teddies, etc. At the height of the debauch, a frosty-eyed general (Stuart Holmes) enters and is revealed as Desnoyers' own nephew; i.e., a cousin of Julio's from the Argentine. Touched by the old man's plight, the officer displays unusual clemency and has him confined to a small, airy dungeon all his own; then, unbuckling his sword, he broaches an especially choice jeroboam of his uncle's champagne for the staff. Julio and Marguerite, in the meantime, continue their marathon renunciation in, of all places, the grotto at Lourdes, where she is nursing her husband, now blind and, of course, totally unaware of her identity.

With a tenacity verging on monomania, Julio still hopes to con his sweetheart back to the ostermoor, but she is adamant. At length, he sickens of the whole enterprise—a process one has anticipated him in by a good half hour—castigates himself as a coward unworthy of her love, and rushes off to enlist. And just in the nick, it may be added, for what scenery hasn't been blasted by the foe has been chewed beyond recognition by the actors. Next to Mary Miles Minter laundering a kitten, nobody in the history of the silent screen could induce mal-de-mer as expertly as Valentino when he bit his knuckles to portray heartbreak.

The ensuing sequence is a bit choppy, occupying itself with Julio's heroism under fire and his parents' vicissitudes, though the only indication we get of the former is a shot of him, in a poilu helmet, fondling a monkey at a first-aid station. (However, the animal may conceivably have been afflicted with rabies.) Papa Desnoyers eludes his captors and visits the young man at the front with news that Marguerite pines for him but is devoting herself unsparingly to the senator, which can hardly be classified as an ingenious plot twist. There obviously remains but one situation to be milked to dramatize the irony of war—a battlefield encounter between Julio and his German cousin—and, blithely skipping over the mechanics of how a general falls into a shell hole in No Man's Land, the scenario maneuvers the relatives into a death grapple. I rather suspect that at this point a hurried story conference was called on the set to debate the propriety of allowing Valentino to be strangled. No doubt it was argued that the spectacle might cause mixed emotions in the audience, and a compromise was evolved wherein, before the outcome is resolved, we whisk to Marguerite's bedroom as she prepares to abandon her husband for Julio. Suddenly her lover's image materializes, suffused with an unearthly radiance, and she realizes the issue is academic. The rest of the picture is a lugubrious wash-up of the incidentals, climaxed by a graveside meeting between the elder Desnoyers and Julio's former upstairs neighbor, the apparition in the fright wig. Their conclusion, as I understood it, was that things were going to be a great deal worse before they became any better, but confidentially I found it hard to keep from whistling as I raced the projectionist to a *bourbonnerie*, around the corner from the Museum. After all, come sunshine or sorrow, it was extremely unlikely I would ever have to see *The Four Horsemen of the Apocalypse* a third time.

With the fatuity of middle age, I imagined I had exorcised the ghost of Valentino for keeps, but in some inexplicable fashion his aura must have clung to my person or otherwise put a hex on me. An evening or so later, my wife exhumed from the attic a Spanish shawl and several filigree combs she had been hoarding until she could get the right offer from a thrift shop. As she was executing an impromptu fandango to the strains of "Siboney," employing a pair of coasters as castanets, I was jealously impelled to demonstrate my superior co-ordination. "Watch this, everybody!" I sang out, flourishing a roll of shelf paper. "My impression of a matador winding himself in his sash, as created by the immortal Rudy Valentino in *Blood and Sand*!" I wrapped one end of the paper around my midriff, ordered a teen-age vassal to pay out some twenty feet and steady the roll, and, with a wild "*Olé!*" spun gyroscopically in her direction. Halfway, I ran full tilt into a peculiar blizzard of white specks and, to weather it, grabbed at a student lamp for support.

I got the lamp, all right, and plenty of time to regret my impetuosity. Lazing around the house with my tweezers, subsequently, probing for slivers of glass, it occurred to me all at once that maybe Valentino used a double in moments of hazard. Maybe I should have, beginning way back around 1921.

Shades of Young Girls
among the Flummery

ONLY an ass, and a knavish one at that, would have the temerity
to compare himself with Boswell, the brothers Goncourt, Rainer
Maria Rilke, or any of the world's other great diarists, but after
thirty-three years of standing around on one foot waiting for a
crumb of recognition, I trust I may be pardoned for blowing my
own horn. Way back in 1920, while *in statu pupillari* at a Rhode
Island lyceum, I kept a journal, briefly, wherein I recorded certain ideals and aspirations, judgments on books and movies that
had impressed me, and appraisals of teachers and relatives who
had not. It is hardly my purpose to dwell here on how trenchant
and shrewd were these comments, how utterly devastating and
yet how accurate; enough to say that if some perceptive critic like
James Gibbons Huneker had been prowling around my bureau
and discovered the diary under the porous-knit union suits where
it lay hidden, he would have unhesitatingly pronounced it a minor
classic. Unfortunately, Huneker seldom got up to New England in
those days and never learned of the existence of the diary prior to
his death. (Whether he learned of it afterward I have, of course,
no way of knowing.) In any case, looking it over a while ago, I

ran across an estimate of a movie I had seen called *The Flapper*, produced by Lewis J. Selznick and starring Olive Thomas. "Coruscating entertainment," I said of it. "Adult fare, replete with Frenchy situations and rib-tickling persiflage. With this production, Hollywood dons long pants. A few more of these, and there is no telling what might happen." Events proved me right. Selznick went bust—the ordinary filmgoer was too crass to appreciate caviar—but his sons vindicated him and made celluloid history. Had I wished to capitalize on my foresight, I, too, might have prospered. Alas, I was a brilliant dreamer, a Mycroft Holmes content to view everything as a chess problem.

Quite recently, in the course of a medical checkup, I was alarmed to find that my masochism count had dropped below the safety level and that I was becoming impervious to cinema flapdoodle. Sure-shot emetics like Kirk Douglas had lost their potency, and even the sight of José Ferrer in *Moulin Rouge*, foreshortened and busily polluting the memory of Toulouse-Lautrec, had aroused no more than the collywobbles one experiences broadside of an oily swell. Faced with such inescapable danger signals, I quickly repaired to the film library of the Museum of Modern Art and outlined my symptoms.

The curator's answer was unequivocal. "This is no time for half measures," he said, his fingertips beating a tattoo on the desk top. From underneath it, where his factotum was quartered, came an answering tattoo. The curator stubbed out his cigarette. "Clear all projection rooms!" he bawled down. "Break out that print of *The Flapper*, produced by Lewis J. Selznick and starring Olive Thomas!" Off in the background, diminuendo, I heard the strident voices of half a dozen Sarah Lawrence graduates relaying the command to the storage vaults. A quarter of an hour later, I was semi-recumbent in a darkened auditorium, my stomach flutter-ing auspiciously and perspiration mantling my forehead. It was a slow, uphill fight, but by the end of the sixth reel I was as panicky as a tenor with a fish-bone in his throat.

Chronologically, the flapper of Olive Thomas antedated by several years that of Clara Bow; the freewheeling galosh and the Stutz Bearcat, the coonskin coat and the débutante slouch were still to emerge as symbols of the Jazz Age, and the theme of Selz-nick's opus, if it had any, was the rebellion ostensibly fermenting in the somewhat younger generation. Casting Miss Thomas as its teen-aged protagonist was, incidentally, sheer dramatic license, for her middy blouse was strained like a balloon jib. The same was true of her schoolmates, a clutch of zestful little breastfuls who must have been recruited from a corset showroom. The fact that they wore Peter Thomsons and hair ribbons and bombarded each other with snowballs didn't upset anyone at the time the picture was current; indeed, it heightened the aura of naughtiness, of Gal-lic spice, that clung to everything surrounding the nickelodeon. Corinne Calvet in a Bikini, nowadays, doesn't have one-third the sizzle of Elaine Hammerstein in a pinafore. Oh, well, two-thirds.

The dramatis personae of *The Flapper* plummet into the open-ing reel with such velocity that the proceedings make little sense at first, but a design presently emerges. Ginger (Olive Thomas), the madcap daughter of Senator King (Warren Cook), has been perturbing everyone in the hamlet of Orange Springs, Florida, with her boisterous antics. Familial patience ends when she takes French leave of some youngsters assigned to her care and goes speedboating with a vacationing freshman from a Northern mili-tary academy, Billy Forbes (Theodore Westman, Jr.). The Senator thereupon packs her off to a misses' seminary—adjoining Billy's school, for plot purposes—whose students are slyly characterized as "limbs of Satan from old family trees." The only evidence of wanton conduct I could detect, however, was a piggish overindulgence in fudge and an occasional typhoon of giggles; on the face of it, Ginger's cronies are as torpid as a moatful of carp, and to alleviate the monotony she breaches the rules and fraternizes with Billy next door. Concurrently, she develops a pash for a mysterious young man named Richard Channing (William P. Carlton, Jr.), who roams the grounds daily on his saddle horse and whom the girls romantically conjecture to be an English lord, a professional gambler, or an actor. (I saw no external evidence to support the last of these, by the way.) "Don't you think he looks like a Greek god?" Ginger observes rapturously to Billy as the stranger canters by. Billy's retort is a squelcher. "He looks like a fried egg to me," he ripostes. Badinage of this stripe has gone out of fashion of late, or possibly I don't know the right teen-agers. It must be two or three years since I've heard anybody declare, "I'm the guy who put salt in the ocean," or "You tell 'em, whalebone, you've been around the ladies."

By maneuvering Billy into a sleigh ride and a consequent upset in the snow, a scene that would prostrate anyone with its antics if he were not already horizontal, Ginger scrapes acquaintance with her idol, falsifies her age, and gets him to invite her to a hop at the local country club. The other bimbos are, of course, oxidized with envy as she struts about waving ostrich fans and bragging of her conquests, and her reputation as a *femme du monde* soars. Unluckily, the headmistress learns of the proposed exploit. She turns up at the dance just as our heroine is holding court around the punch bowl; Channing, miffed at his public embarrassment, refers to Ginger in her hearing as a pinfeathered saphead, which compounds the debacle; and on being haled back to school, she theatrically presses a cluster of lilies to her bosom and prepares to hang herself from a chandelier. Meanwhile, the plot—to employ a courtly synonym—has been proliferating in another and more melodramatic direction. A student named Hortense (Katherine Johnston), described as "a moth among the butterflies," has been in league with one Tom Morran, alias the Eel (Arthur Johnston), to rob the school safe. The valuables contained there—as far as I could see, a string of beads and some women's dresses—hardly warrant being kept under lock and key, but anyway Ginger spies the couple descending a ladder with two suitcases and forgets her suicidal impulse. Despite Hortense's disappearance, the premise is advanced that nobody links her with the caper; the headmistress, clearly someone who lives in a world of fantasy if she keeps clothing in a safe, hushes up the affair on understandable grounds, and her charges start packing for their midterm vacation. Just as the picture showed every sign of being moribund, and I was massaging my knee to obviate the nut-cracking sound so embarrassing in a projection room, the story shuddered convulsively and lumbered off again. I would have followed suit if I could have got my knee back into its socket.

Hortense and the Eel, a dissolve reveals, are bivouacked in a New York hotel, in whose lobby they accidentally see Channing, and they now originate the notion of making Ginger the goat for the robbery. Since Channing does not know them, and since, moreover, the theft has been hushed up, there isn't the slightest trace of logic in any of this; I'm merely repeating what danced across the screen. The heavies dispatch a telegram luring Ginger to their suite, where Hortense confides that she and the Eel were eloping when her schoolmate last saw them. Reassured, Ginger is persuaded to tarry the night, and shortly meets Channing in the dining room. He is also bound for Orange Springs, by a rare coincidence, and paternally tries to induce her to take the same train, but nothing happens, just as it has been happening with dizzying regularity all along. In the middle of the night Ginger is awakened at gun point by the confederates, given the suitcases containing the boodle, and ordered to hide them in Orange Springs until they reclaim them. You or I might regard this as rather eccentric behavior; Ginger, however, treats it with aplomb and, after they bolt, settles down, fascinated, to examine the suitcases. Hidden in the clothing is a packet of sultry love letters from the Eel to Hortense, which, announces a succession of titles, give Ginger a delicious idea: "A complete outfit for a woman of experience . . . She might borrow it and vamp Channing . . . She would go home with a manufactured past."

Well, sir, if you think the foregoing is a wee bit daft, the rest of it is more Surrealist than *Le Chien Andalou* or one of those comic-strip nightmares Little Nemo used to get from eating Welsh rabbits. Down in Orange Springs, a staid party of townswomen is convened at the King home, buzzing over the teacups, when Ginger draws up in a calash, sporting a Duchess of Devonshire hat trimmed with osprey feathers, a hobble skirt, and opera-length gloves, and flaunting a court chamberlain's baton. How this finery had found its way into the school safe, unless the headmistress was in the habit of impersonating Lady Teazle after lights-out, is the only suspenseful element I saw anywhere in *The Flapper*. "Howdy, Gushy, old top," Ginger drawls to a neighbor. "How's everything in the little old town?" To their intense alarm—and when those early screen actors registered alarm, the camera tri-

pod shook—the ladies hear the girl confess that she has been leading a double life in New York, gallivanting around till 4 A.M., etc.
etc. To intensify the atmosphere of dementia, Billy Forbes rockets
in, reacts in horror to the metamorphosis, and races off to berate
Channing for having led his sweetheart astray. As the whole thing
deteriorates into bedlam, with Senator King distractedly vowing
to kill Ginger's seducer, the brat restores the clothes to the valises
and endeavors to ship them by railway express to the New York
police. The freight agent, suspicious, fetches a detective, who
promptly arrests her. (It wouldn't have surprised me in the least,
by then, if she had arrested *him*.) A mighty hue and cry ensues
in the King household when she is brought back, everyone bel-
lowing and fainting like sixty, but eventually the plainclothesman
recognizes the handwriting in the love letters as that of the Eel—
am I going too fast for you?—and the mystery is solved. To round
matters off neatly, the Eel and Hortense show up to retrieve their
swag and are whisked off to pokey, and the last shot, prefaced by a
newspaper headline reading, "ORANGE SPRINGS SOCIAL WELFARE
WORKERS HORRIFIED OVER SOFT DRINK DISSIPATION," shows Ginger and Billy devouring sodas and cooing to each other.

It was in a state of acute vertigo, as though I had been rotated
in a cocktail shaker, that I left the Museum to buy a stirrup cup
at Schrafft's for my daughter, herself a student at a New England
academy and entraining that afternoon for the fall semester. Over
the parfaits, I listened to a breathless recapitulation of her day.
She had picked up a bargain autograph of Marlon Brando at a
Sixth Avenue pornographer's, priced a star sapphire at Tiffany's
and given the salesperson my phone number, and, cannily sensing
that prices were at their peak, charged several thousand dollars'

worth of gowns suitable for embassy functions. "And what did *you* do today?" she asked solicitously, sponging a tiny bead of fudge from my cravat. On the theory that Ginger's misadventures might furnish a moral lesson, I began recounting the plot of *The Flapper*. Halfway through, she broke in nervously. "Look, I won't hear of you coming to the train," she said. "You're going home to bed this second." With the aid of a mysterious bystander who could have been an English lord, a professional gambler, or an actor but who turned out to be the manager, I was loaded into a calash and sent home. She must have got back to school safely, unless she took off for Orange Springs. You never know which way these modern kids'll jump. Why, when I was her age, I already kept a journal that frankly— But there I go, blowing my own horn.

About the Author

SIDNEY JOSEPH PERELMAN was born on February 1, 1904, in Brooklyn, New York, the only child of working-class Russian Jewish immigrants with strong socialist sympathies. Soon after his birth, the family moved to Rhode Island, where his father opened a dry goods store in Providence. After the dry goods store failed, the family then purchased a chicken farm in nearby Norwood, Rhode Island. That enterprise, too, would eventually fail. In 1921, Perelman entered Brown University, where he met Nathanael West and became the editor of *The Brown Jug*, the campus humor magazine. Falling three credits short of his college degree after flunking Trigonometry, he left Brown to take a job as a cartoonist with *Judge* magazine, which also provided a venue for Perelman's short humorous sketches. In 1929, Perelman and West's sister, Laura, married. In 1931, accompanied by Laura, Perelman traveled to Hollywood to work on the Marx Brothers films *Monkey Business* and *Horse Feathers*. Over the next eleven years, he and Laura returned to Hollywood numerous times, often working together as screenwriters. In 1932, the Perelmans (with West) purchased an eighty-three-acre farm in Bucks County, Pennsylvania (Perelman gathered his humorous pieces on the exasperations of country living in his 1947 collection *Acres and Pains*). In all, Perelman wrote more than 450 humorous sketches and satires, many of them published in *The New Yorker.* His long association with the magazine began in 1930 and continued until his death. During his lifetime, his sketches and satires were gathered in almost two dozen volumes, among them *Strictly from Hunger* (1937), *Crazy Like a Fox* (1946), *Listen to the Mocking Bird* (1949), *The Ill-Tempered Clavichord* (1952), *The Road to Miltown* (1957), *The Rising Gorge* (1961), and *Chicken Inspector No. 23* (1966). In addition to his short prose pieces, Perelman wrote or cowrote several Broadway plays, including *Walk a Little Faster* (1932), *One Touch of Venus* (1943), and *The Beauty Part* (1962). He won an Oscar for Best Adapted Screenplay for *Around the World in Eighty Days* (1956), sharing the award with cowriters John Farrow and James Poe. Perelman died of a heart attack on October 17, 1979, in his apartment at the Gramercy Park Hotel.

This book is set in 10-point Freight Text, a serif typeface issued by Darden Foundry, Brooklyn, NY, and created by its founding designer Joshua Darden, who published his first typeface at the age of fifteen. The Freight font superfamily was inspired the eighteenth-century Dutch school of typefaces, including the old-style designs cut by Joan Michaël Fleischman (Germany-Holland) and Miklós Tótfalusi (Hungary) and the later designs of William Caslon (UK). Initially released in 2005, the Freight Text family is notable for its multiple weights, widths, and optical sizes—comprising 156 fonts in all.

Chapter titles and display type are set in Kepler, modeled after modern eighteenth-century typefaces with a hint of old-style proportion. It was released in 1996 by award-winning American typographer Robert Slimbach in 1990 for Adobe Systems

Text designer and composition by Gopa & Ted2, Inc. Albuquerque, NM. Cover design by Kimberly Glyder. Printing and binding by Lakeside Book Company.